BLOOD
SWEAT &
CHARITY

THE ULTIMATE CHARITY
CHALLENGE HANDBOOK

NICK STANHOPE

PUBLISHED BY EYE
BOOKS

Blood Sweat & Charity
1st Edition
September 2005

Published by Eye Books Ltd
Colemore Farm
Colemore Green
Bridgnorth
Shropshire
Tel/fax: +44 (0) 845 4508870
website: www.eye-books.com

ISBN: 1903070414

British Library Cataloguing in Publication Data
A catalogue record for this book is available from the British Library

Cover photo: Jono Felix
Cover design: Peter Ashley and Michael Stanhope

Acknowledgments

The idea behind this charity challenge handbook is to help you have an amázing experience and achieve something really worthwhile. To do this I have shared my own experience and also drawn on that of hundreds of others who have offered endless help, support and advice. Many of these people appear in the book, giving snippets of advice or sharing their expertise. Many others have been behind the scenes and I would like to thank them for everything they have done.

Mum, Dad and Alex, you've been so supportive in lots of different ways, and I will always be grateful for everything you did during the Anti-Slavery International project. This formative expedition was also made possible by the support and generosity of so many people. I would like to say a special thank you to all the Stanhopes, Parkers, Stanyers, Hadmans, Gowlands, O'Callaghans and Polonskys and, of course, Jess. Nick McConnell, my flatmate during most of the writing of Blood, Sweat & Charity, was a sounding board for everything from sponsorship forms to training shoes and offered great advice throughout. Rob Hadman and Rebecca Gowland, the best couple in the world and also fine challenge companions, and Duncan Brown, Jonny Polonsky and Jono Felix have been the main protagonists in my own projects and hugely supportive and influential. Peter Ashley, your generosity and skills have been much appreciated. Also thank you to Alix Owens and Trisha Talep for your time and help; and to Martin Collier, friend and mentor.

Kids, a great charity providing unparalleled services to disabled children and their families and my employer through most of the researching and writing of the book, have been very understanding and encouraging. The Royal Geographic Society and particularly Shane Warner, have been very supportive and helped to give me a platform. Ollie Steeds and iNOMAD, a great forum for sharing expeditionary and creative experiences, have given me time, knowledge and contacts. The British Library and its helpful staff have made accessing resources very painless.

Finally, but certainly not least of all, thanks to Dan Hiscocks, my publisher and friend, who has remained true to his mission to produce books of real social value through Eye Books. Without his encouragement, backing and contributions, this handbook would never have been written, let alone published. To Fiona Hiscocks, a big thank you for all your support, which has been so important for both of us.

Contents

Physical Challenge (Section D) 141

Organisation (Section E) 183

Documenting (Section F) 207

Index & Reference 219

Challenge Profiles ....

How To Use This Book

Blood, Sweat & Charity will provide you with information and inspiration, giving you the tools, both practical and psychological, to take on a remarkable challenge. Some may come to this guide with just a vague idea about what they want. Others may have already booked a place in a marathon event, registered with their favourite charity or be in the midst of planning their own adventure.

The needs of these different groups may vary but the book is designed with them all in mind. It is divided into three main stages:

Are you starting from scratch? A blank sheet, waiting to be convinced of what a charity challenge could do for you? Do you like the idea of doing something for charity, having an adventure and getting fit, but don't really know why?

If yes, then turn to section A.

Are you convinced of the worth of a charity challenge and set on taking one on? Do you know that this is for you, but want to know where to look first and how to make all the important choices? Which charity? What challenge? Motivated, but undecided?

If yes, then turn to section B.

Are you registered for an event? Or, having found a charity, a route and a means, do you now need the information to raise mountains of cash and get seriously fit? Do you need to know how to plan and organise your own challenge expedition?

If yes, then turn to sections C to F.

The guide covers the journey from that first idea to a complete project. Some of you may have already started that journey. However, even in those sections that deal with decisions you have already taken or ideas already thought through, you will find advice and suggestions that can only add to what you already know. My hope is that you will be able to benefit from what has been not only my own journey but that of hundreds of thousands of people whose lives have been changed and enriched by taking on their own extraordinary challenges.

KEY

 Remember icon – Look out for these important points.

 Website icon – Further information can be found on the adjacent topic on the Blood, Sweat & Charity website: www.eye-books.com/BloodSweatandCharity

Special Pages – You will find these special features highlighted with a green background. They provide information on important topics that can be looked at in isolation or as part of the relevant chapter.

Challenge Profiles – Case studies of a broad range of challenges are dotted around the book, highlighted in green.

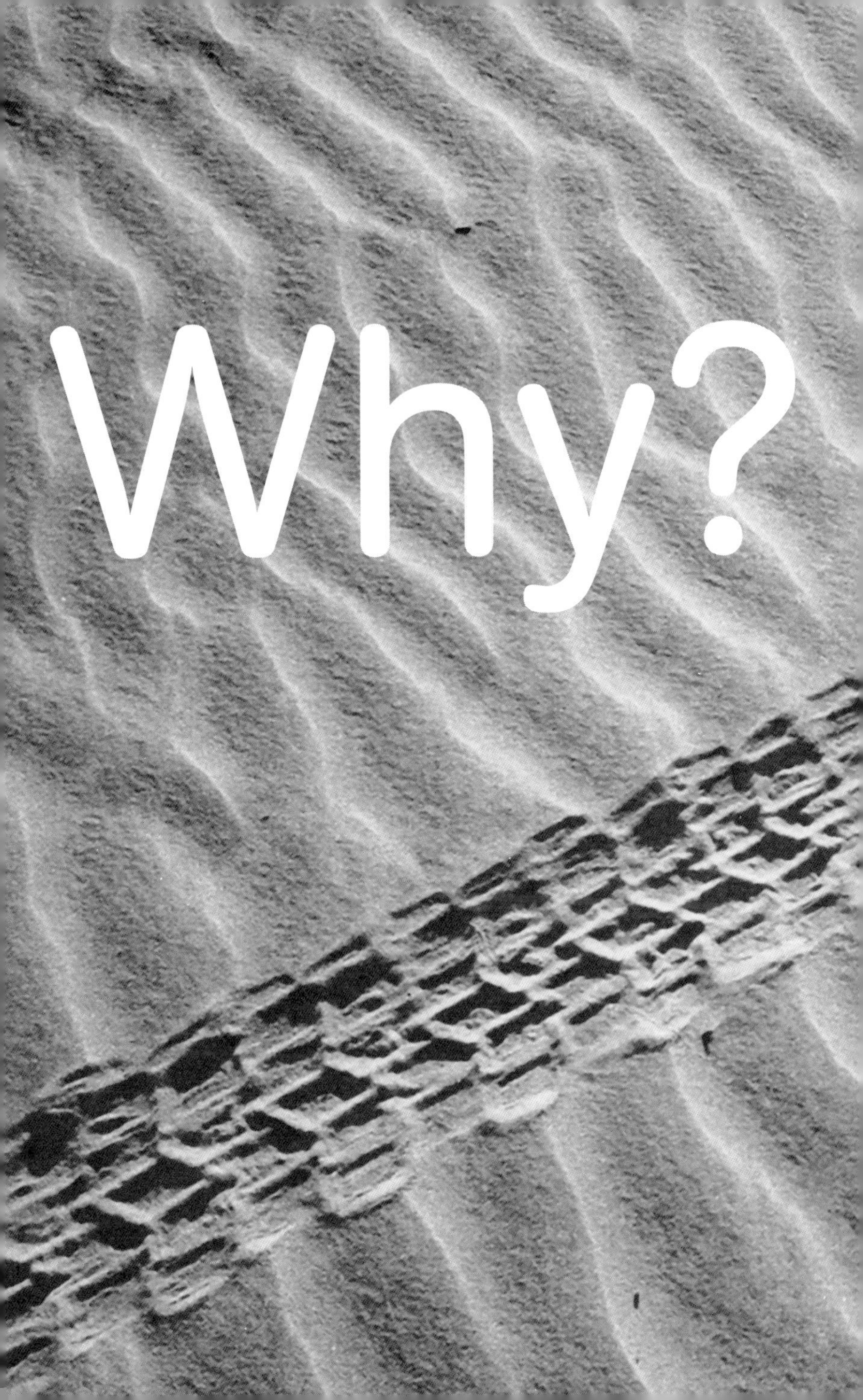
Why?

Charity challenges are powerful vehicles for realising personal goals and raising vast sums of money for charity. They inspire goodwill, raise awareness of important issues, help people find outlets for loss or dissatisfaction, stir camaraderie among strangers and bring out the best in people. But it is a strange concept, swapping blood and sweat for charity, and one that needs looking at. To really feel as if you are doing something worthwhile, with all the sacrifices that tough charity challenges involve, you should be convinced of exactly what they are, what they can achieve and whether they are for you.

Why?

What is a charity challenge?

A charity challenge is an exchange. You put yourself through an extraordinary physical and mental test and in return those around you, and those who you have affected and inspired, contribute money and attention to your chosen cause. A worthy charity challenge is anything that represents the limits of your endurance and the result of long-term commitment. It is the culmination of a period of dedication and, vitally, passion. In this way it can be a million different things to a million different people.

On 20th of January, 2004, we were carrying our bikes through the thick, bright desert of northern Sudan. Around us was nothing. Ahead of us was a night in a hut and a plate of over-boiled beans. My temperature had reached 41° the evening before, Rob probably had cholera and we had run out of money. Every time we climbed back on our bikes and faced into the Saharan wind that blew from Cairo to Khartoum, we would find ourselves sinking further back into the desert. Our tyres would slip effortlessly through the sand and the bikes would not move.

With a sip of warm, chlorinated water and a scowl, we would lift our bikes onto our shoulders and carry on towards Europe. Mentally, it was excruciating. The wind beat us down relentlessly and the vastness of the desert never hinted at a change of luck. Half of every moment was spent thinking about where we would rather have been. The other half of every moment was spent being amazed that we could do this, week after week, month after month. This feeling, plus the satisfaction of having raised so much money and the time we had spent with Anti-Slavery International projects all over Africa, is something that I will be able to keep forever. Every challenge I've done, from a day's walking to 6 months' cycling, has made me feel the same and everybody has the chance to experience this.

Nick & Rob walking across the North Sudanese desert (photo: Jonny Plonsky)

What's in it for me?

For the vast majority of us, daily life is a 99% risk-free experience. Physically, we may or may not go to the gym, run round the park or cycle to work, but either way we never have to reach into our deepest reserves and rely solely on our will power and physical limits.

Regardless of your age, fitness, job, income, marital status, background, politics, beliefs, commitments or responsibilities, you can take on a challenge, complete it and in doing so gain massive rewards, personally and for a worthwhile cause. Crossing the finish line after a 10,000-mile trek or a 5-kilometre run is an incredible, life-changing feeling that everyone can experience. This is an opportunity to push your limits and demonstrate a commitment to other people's needs as well as your own.

In the short term, there is the euphoria of discovering your hidden capabilties and witnessing the contribution you have made to something constructive and worthwhile. In the long term you benefit from improved confidence, self-esteem and self-reliance, as well as an awareness of other people's lives, the needs of society and your own capacity to play a part in addressing them. The moment of ecstasy that

"The cycling expedition was a great personal challenge - a test of my physical resources and mental willpower. Before I left, I wasn't sure I could do it, but successfully completing my challenge has given me a sense of self-confidence that is still with me."

Colin Brooks, looking back at his cycling challenge from Cusco to Machu Pichu for ActionAid

follows this incredibly tough experience is not simply a rush of endorphins from the exercise, but a profound realisation

"One of the most common problems with training programmes is motivation. In this sense a charity challenge is ideal. It gives you a focus, it helps you improve your diet and it makes you feel that what you are doing is really worthwhile. Most participants start to look for the next challenge almost as soon as they have finished the first."

Men's Fitness

of your own power as a human being. Too many things make us feel ordinary, unglamorous and unsatisfied. This realisation of self-worth makes all that rubbish seem as irrelevant as it should be.

To complete a charity challenge you will probably have to get into the best shape of your life. By providing an ideal focus for your training, a specific challenge will motivate you to eat and exercise in a way that you may never have been able to do before. If you follow a gradual, sensible and considered programme then you will look, feel and be significantly healthier. You will also develop a large number of skills and personal assets that will make you more competent and more employable.

Motivation, organisation, commitment, ambition, awareness and passion will be required in bucket loads for your challenge. The fundraising work that you will be undertaking demands ingenuity and involves developing communication and marketing skills. Last and least of all, you will look really tough in front of your friends and have something to impress strangers with at drinks parties!

There are also times in life when you are made to feel outside your social comfort zone. For some this may be inspired by a tangible moment, from the death of someone close to you, to an article about human rights violations in Guantanamo Bay, to an event like the South-East Asian tsunami disaster. For others, there might always have been a nagging discomfort, a feeling of helplessness amongst all the endless problems, a feeling that only massive changes to how things work could make a difference to the big issues that confront us in the 21st century. What an endurance fundraising project enables you to do is connect these feelings with that longing for a challenge, an adventure and a means of self-discovery.

Whatever your motivations you will ultimately achieve worthwhile results— to give something back, to accomplish something meaningful, to make a difference to something that affects you, and to let people know about an issue that you feel strongly about. Adventure, personal growth, escape and pride are your rewards, which can be realised especially when combined with a passion and enthusiasm to contribute.

What's in it for charity?

Charity challenges, when they are done well, are hugely inspirational. The more committed you are, physically and emotionally, the more you will inspire people.

The more extraordinary your efforts, the more seriously you take the project, the more time and resources that you put into organising it, the more professionally you conduct yourself throughout, and the more you take advantage of opportunities to raise the profile of your cause, the more you will inspire people. All of this can be channelled into producing fantastic benefits for your chosen cause.

As a professional fundraiser my motivations lie in the voluntary sector and in the power of awareness and information. I can help you create a project that raises huge amounts of money, makes thousands more people aware of crucial issues and moves others to take on similar challenges and make a commitment to charitable giving. After a recent Charities Aid Foundation study (Inside Rsearch, Oct, 2004) showed that 40% of the population know they can afford to double the amount of money given to charity every week and you have the ability to mobilise this latent generosity.

In the wake of the terrible Asian tsunami disaster in December 2004, the reaction of the public was simply awesome. In their millions, people gave vastly more than they normally would.

Has this left them unable to eat or buy clothes for their children? Of course not. We are a wealthy society that has very high levels of disposable income. That a proportion of this income was immediately mobilised to contribute hundreds of millions of pounds within a matter of weeks is testament, of course, to the scale of the disaster and the immediacy of the need in the affected areas. However, it also demonstrates what happens when people's sympathies are deeply touched. A brilliantly organised challenge event is a powerful way of persuading people to support charities—your commitment is their inspiration.

People give to causes that they are somehow attached to, that they feel are in some way part of their lives. In the wake of disasters or tragic events, such as the September 11th terrorist attacks in 2001, the response of the public is conditioned by the degree to which they feel affected by what has happened. In this, case the cultural proximity of

"While most of us freely admit that we could give more to charity, few of us actually do. For many of us giving is simply not a priority and it's up to charities to find even more powerful ways of persuading people of the value of their work."

Cathy Pharoah, Director of Research at the Charities Aid Foundation

Manhattan and the vivid images that confronted the public may have helped galvanise the immensely generous response. The death of Princess Diana in 1997 incited an enormous injection of funds into the Princess Diana Memorial Fund and into the causes close to her heart. In this case, the public did not respond to a particular need, but instead they gave as an outlet for the grief they felt for losing someone who was part of their lives. Similarly, in May 2005, the pop star Kylie Minogue was diagnosed with breast cancer and the public's adoration of this celebrity resulted in a huge increase in contributions to cancer charities around the world and a flood of new awareness of the importance of self-checks. In Britain, medical charities receive fantastic support from patients and their friends and families. Similarly, people are more likely to support an international cause in countries that they have visited, pet owners more likely to contribute to the RSPCA, and so on.

All of this means that as someone who is already a part of hundreds or thousands of people's lives, either directly or indirectly, you have the power to mobilise their sympathies and their generosity. You also have the potential through the media, events and awareness work, to bring your cause into the public eye. Make your cause a part of people's lives and you will achieve incredible things for charity.

Addressing the Issues: charities & money

Some people have reservations about giving money to charities, and doubts about where the funds end up. Donors often worry that their money is being swallowed by a huge administrative machine and that ultimately very little of it ends up directly dealing with the problem on the ground. For almost half of the public surveyed (Davis Smith, 1997) this was the factor that most dampened their generous instincts: they were convinced by the needs but did not feel that large organisations, burdened by bureaucratic structures, were effective in addressing them directly.

Over the last twenty years, administrative costs and salaries have remained constant, while the impact and importance of the voluntary sector has increased dramatically and the sector still relies upon a generous and trusting public. Firstly, not a penny is spent lightly by charities. There are no costly employee perks, business class flights to Addis Ababa or meals out "on the company card" in voluntary organisations. Not only are charities "not for profit", but they are also not for those looking for high salaries and cushy pensions.

Charities have become more professional about their work and their operational structures. This has considerably reduced waste in the sector. By employing a team of professional fundraisers, by formalising the finance structures and by taking the best bits out of the private sector, charities have become more efficient, more effective and considerably more accountable. Endemic incompetence has been replaced by an overriding professionalism and therefore money invested in charities does not get lost in a giant machine.

Beyond this professional structure there is still a very strong and very kind heart to voluntary organisations. You are investing in businesses, but ones that operate with the most ethical awareness and the greatest degree of social conscience. From their employment

Charities are much more efficient than most people think: on average they spend 82p in the £1 on their cause, and just 8p on management and admin and 8p on fundraising. Investing areas like finance, IT and fundraising is vital because it makes it possible for donors to track where money is being spent, makes the charity more efficient and secures its future. Employing professions means fundraising is more targeted and fewer resources are wasted.

Emma Maier - Features and Supplements Editor

Third Sector (weekly news magazine for the voluntary sector)

to their environmental policies these organisations set very high standards which can only have a positive influence on the rest of the economy.

Of course, these reservations may go even deeper, and may challenge the very existence of charitable organisations within society. It cannot be taken for granted that charity is the answer to society's afflictions. Perhaps charities would not be necessary if we took on all our social and community responsibilities. This means that giving money to charity can become a way of replacing the consideration and energy that should be spent on society's problems.

However, in our current system charities and NGOs work to tackle issues that rarely get the attention they deserve and never get the resources they need. Without their existence the lives of millions of people around the world would be considerably worse and that is a fact.

But are they ultimately progressive and constructive beyond a temporary bandage effect? Directly, charities encourage an awareness of and an emotional investment in important issues. They hope that this will lead to a financial investment, but even if it does not, people are still more aware of issues and so more likely to take them into account when they make their daily decisions. Some charities, such as Scope, work to improve the lives of disabled people marginalised within society through massive awareness and public education campaigns. This hugely positive and long-term social investment will be felt for generations.

Charities also encourage companies to be more responsible: environmentally, ethically and within their communities. This, combined with an amazing growth in popular demand for a corporate conscience, has meant that most companies feel obliged to take on these responsibilities.

Business in the Community is a key example of how charities and not-for-profit organisations work to inspire, challenge and support business in improving its impact on society. This organisation works with 700 companies directly and 1,600 more through their programmes and campaigns. This constitutes 1 in 5 UK employees. Along with their global partners, BITC influence over 15 million employees. Through BITC and other similar enabling organisations, as well as through thousands of direct relationships between charites and companies, collaboration and progress is becoming the norm, rather than tension and cynicism.

Companies have been forced by charities, and by an increasingly aware public and sensitive shareholder, to make genuine commitments to their communities, at home and abroad.

Indirectly, the existence of organisations that aim not to make shareholders richer but to improve the lives of the disadvantaged is crucial to our faith in mankind. The modern voluntary sector has not just evolved more professional structures, it has also learned from the mistakes of the past. Victims of homelessness are not just given a bowl of soup and told to stay out of trouble. There is recognition of their emotional and practical needs. Disabled people are no longer simply cared for in specialist environments, hidden and marginalised. Full inclusion is now the goal, pursued at every level, from children's play, to higher education, to employment. These modern solutions are not just plasters and palliatives.

Addressing the Issues: charities & challenges

There is some scepticism about charity challenges and at the motivations of those who undertake them, their place within charity fundraising and their impact on communities around the world.

Problem 1

Charity challenges are just a means of getting funding for adventures. They are only done for personal reasons to gain personal benefits.

Yes, there are personal benefits to charity challenges. The physical achievement is primarily an intensely personal one. Furthermore, they can involve travelling through beautiful landscapes and visiting exotic tourist destinations. Participants complete their challenges having had an experience of a lifetime and done something they will never forget. However, all of the personal rewards rely upon sacrifices – of everyday priorities and commitments, of time to train and fundraise, of energy and pain to complete the challenge.

Moreover, you can see that these are underpinned by an overwhelming sense of achieving something worthwhile.

If challenges have not been hard and have been predominantly "fun", then this may rest on the conscience of the participant for picking an undemanding challenge. But with the right information and advice this will not happen, and dedication and endurance will be exchanged for support and sponsorship.

Problem 2

Charity challenges do not engage with the charity or the cause in any other way than a functional one. The charity is a final and unfelt addition to a personal challenge.

This is a common issue, but not one that needs to continue. This guide promotes examples of best practice because the most rewarding and successful aspect of undertaking a challenge is the positive charitable results that it produces. These results are multiplied if you have an emotional attachment to your cause and when this passion becomes reflected in

everything that you do for your charity. This relationship, which can develop during the course of a challenge project, can last a lifetime and yield profound and long-lasting mutual benefits. More and more charities, operators and participants are making the work of the charity an integral part of challenges.

Participants in Norwood challenges (seen here) raising money for the charity's work with disabled and disadvantaged members of Jewish communities, are accompanied by some of the disabled service users that their efforts are supporting. This has huge mutual benefits, offering the disabled young people a chance to participate in a very rewarding inclusive team experience. At the same time, the fundraising participants can develop a close relationship with these service users and with the cause as a whole.

➠ "It's hard work and I have to get really fit, but I love being able to meet new people, make new friends and see some amazing scenery in different parts of the world."

Julian Primhok, a resident at Norwood's Ravenswood Village

➠ "The final leg of the challenges are always amazing, when the whole group gets together and sets off towards the finish. Then we have a huge party, where we can mix and have fun."

Philip Lee, Ravenswood resident

➠ "Being able to meet and spend time with some of the young disabled people from the Ravenswood Village made a huge impression on me - I will never forget the whole experience."

Norwood Challenge Participant

Residents and staff from Norwood's Ravenswood Village on a cycling challenge through Israel in 2004.

Karen Darke independently planned an inclusive challenge from Kyrgyzstan to Pakistan by bicycle and handcycle. Karen intertwined the challenge and her chosen charity to demonstrate the potential of disabled people as well as raise vital funds for Scotland's Alternative Skiers, who provide opportunities for disabled people to access the mountains and different activities. Every aspect of Karen's expedition reflected its aims: to make society more aware of the abilities of disabled people and more inclusive of their needs and demands.

➤➤ This is a charity which helped me to access the mountains again after breaking my back in a climbing accident and becoming paralysed. It was also very important for me to raise awareness of disability and inclusion in the UK. By undertaking a successful expedition with an inclusive team that attracted some positive media attention, we were able to raise the profile of what disabled explorers can achieve."

Karen Darke, Learning and Development Consultant, 34.
Read a full profile of Karen's challange on page 172.

Karen Darke and one of her team mates on the challenge

Problem 3

When done in big, poorly organised groups, charity challenges often make use of adventurous or extreme environments without any consideration for the needs and sensitivities of that environment and its communities.

This is a prevalent criticism, but one that is fast disappearing as charities and operators are now addressing it. These are some the examples from around the industry, which are becoming the rule rather the exception:

▶ Charity Challenge only take groups of up to 25 and have strict environmental and ethical guidelines, aiming to keep their impact to an absolute minimum. They have also recently launched Community Challenges in which the sponsored challenge consists of building and regeneration work. (see page 140)

▶ An increasing number of overseas challenge packages, pioneered by Mencap's Project Renew, include a period of volunteering for a local regeneration project as part of overseas trek itineraries.

▶ 2% of the proceeds from CARE International's UK challenges are donated to organisations working to maintain and improve the surrounding environment and also to local community projects.

▶ On international expeditions Across the Divide only employ local guides and donate a proportion of funds to local projects.

Conclusion

The concept of a charity challenge is very sound and one that can stand up to cynicism and criticism because, if the ideal is abided by, there can only be very worthwhile results. The logic is thus: your extraordinary effort and remarkable achievement show a huge commitment to

A team of local guides employed by Across the Divide in China

something constructive, which in turn inspires others to support you and your cause.

Excuses, Excuses

So what's stopping you? Maybe nothing, in which case read on into Section B and start to consider some of the choices that await you. However, you may still have some personal reservations that make you believe these challenges are not for you.

⏸ I'm not physically up to a test of endurance

This is the first reaction of many people to the idea of a serious physical challenge. Pushing your body to its limits is not everyone's cup of tea. In fact, aerobic exhaustion, muscle fatigue and self-imposed emotional collapse are not really anyone's cup of tea. The nature of a physical challenge is not muscular or aerobic but, ultimately, psychological. There will be training that you will not want to do, sacrifices that you will have to keep making and emotional barriers that you will have to surpass. All of them will have to be overcome in your head before you can progress, but ultimately everyone is capable of them.

⏸ I don't have enough time in my busy life

In our lives, we choose to prioritise one thing over another. Make this challenge a priority, and a permanent fixture in your diary. Set out what you want to do and give it all the time that you can. Break every aspect of the project down into manageable chunks and it will become much more feasible and exciting. As time goes on the challenge will become a natural part of your life and your schedule. You will never regret making the commitment or making the time for it.

⏸ I have far too many responsibilities

Everyone who has achieved something remarkable for charity has made serious sacrifices, whether personal, financial or physical. How you view the prospect of these sacrifices may change as you begin to see the potential rewards, but for now remember that the level of sacrifice is up to you. No one has too many commitments to find eight hours a week to train for a marathon.

The support you receive from family, friends and workmates will be tremendous and your ability to mobilise that support is a major reason for taking this on in the first place.

⏸ Am I really going to make a difference?

If you feel strongly about a cause then you will probably also understand its complexities. You will know that a cure for cancer will not be found on the back of a £2,000 challenge fundraiser, nor will Third World poverty be dented by your efforts. However, you aren't aiming to do either of these things. No one person can find a cure for cancer or take on global inequality. By taking on an inspirational endurance fundraiser you are raise money for an organisation that works to make life better for people and raising awareness of a cause that needs

A delighted London Marathon runner for Whizz-Kidz celebrates crossing the finishing line after months of training and preparation

attention. Also remember that the choice of charity is completely yours which means that the type of impact you have on a particular issue is up to you.

➡ I don't know anyone with money to sponsor me

When you look around at your family, friends and contacts you may well not see many people who could be approached for money. This is frustrating, but not as important as it might seem. A list of people who work in pubs, shops and factories, with a smattering of teachers and civil servants, may not offer the disposable income to give you substantial funding, but they all open doors to opportunities. Small local businesses, associations, clubs, schools and unions can form the basis of an enormously successful fundraising campaign and very receptive targets for spreading awareness. Ultimately, these

sources can often be more rewarding than envelopes full of cheques sent in from wealthy friends and relatives.

You may also be wary of pestering people. Don't be. You have decided to make a sacrifice of time, energy and effort. You are going to put yourself through physical and emotional tests. This is an inspiring thing to do and you have the right to ask people to support you. The more you demonstrate your enthusiasm and commitment to your challenge and your charity, the easier it will be to ask and the more you will be supported.

➡ I don't have enough motivation to do it

Motivation is not something that can be quantified and analysed. It is intensely personal. But, you are reading this. Something has made you pick it up off the shelf and that curiosity is a sign that a part of you wants to challenge yourself. The hardest motivational moments will come during the challenge itself. At this point you will have to completely rely on yourself. These are the times that offer the greatest rewards, and when you'll surprise yourself most.

Why don't I just give money or commit to volunteering?

A charity challenge does not have to be a replacement for contributing to charity in other ways. At their best, they are part of a commitment to addressing an issue that means something to you. They can also be combined with volunteering and giving to make the most of this contribution.

A central motivation of taking on a charity challenge project is that you want to have a greater impact than your own financial resources allow. To be passionate enough about something to devote a month, six months or a year and endless reserves of energy to it draws attention to the issue and also inspires others to become more concerned with the cause. Your dedication and commitment are the perfect advertisement for its importance, which gives you the opportunity to inspire new relationships between your supporters and your charity.

As a challenge participant you are making sacrifices by volunteering your time to training and fundraising, and by shifting your priorities to achieve your charity challenge goals. These sacrifices are worthwhile and valuable.

Choices

Once you have decided that you want to commit to a charity challenge the road ahead is full of possibilities. There are hundreds of thousands of charities in need of your support and an endless number of challenges to be taken on in their name. There may always have been a charity that you wanted to support, or a challenge that you have been desperate to complete, which will give your choices a head start. Whatever your preconceptions are, give these decisions some consideration, because you will have to be convinced of their worth every step of the way.

Choice 1

Choosing your challenge

There are two ways of approaching your choice of challenge. The first involves putting total faith in your imagination, ambition and bravery and then relying upon your commitment. This will allow you to take on absolutely anything, as no matter what the physical demands entail, you will be prepared to dedicate any amount of time to conditioning and equipping yourself with a far more advanced cardiovascular capacity and muscular endurance than you could ever have imagined possessing. On top of this you may be willing to give yourself time to develop skills, train for qualifications and accumulate experience in certain fields, as well as raise enormous amounts of money over a long period of time and become intimate with the complexities of your cause. If there is something that attracts you to this then go for it – you will never regret it.

The second involves taking a more realistic account of a whole range of factors, from your current physical condition to your future commitments. These factors form something of an equation, the results of which form a category of challenges that you will be capable of undertaking. The beauty of this, however, is that some of the original factors are up to you, so change these and the result becomes more exciting, more ambitious and more challenging.

Your Challenge Capacity

The Constants

Current Fitness Level

Where you are now dictates where you can realistically be in 2, 4, 6 or 12 months' time. As a guide, most experts agree that someone with no fitness regime or record of training would need between 18 months and 2 years to reach a level of fitness that would enable them to complete a marathon. From this it could take a further 12 months to reach the capacity required to complete an ultramarathon of 100 miles in a day. (more examples on pages 32-35)

General Health

The emphasis here is on health rather than age, because men and women of almost any age have realized some of the most remarkable physical feats on the planet. Basically, if you have any kind of condition that will put a ceiling on your physical condition then this is unavoidable. Your doctor is the only person that can provide you with this guidance.

Ability

Choosing a challenge involves choosing an activity. Many of these come naturally, such as running and cycling, but others, such as kayaking or mountaineering, need years of practice and experience.

The Variables

Preparation Period

Think about when you want to take this challenge and therefore how much time you are going to give yourself to equip yourself for its demands.

Level of Commitment

The time that you can give to prepare will dictate the extent of your ambition. Training regimes for marathons start at around 5 hours a week and begin a minimum of 6 months before the event; for an ascent of Kilimanjaro around 3 hours a week and for a full triathlon about 6 hours a week. All the variables depend upon your targets for the completion of the challenge. On top of this you should consider the length of time you can commit to the actual challenge, which could be anything from an hour to a year.

Mental Toughness

You might consider this to be a constant, but the vast majority of people who have taken on hard physical challenges for the first time surprise themselves by their capacity to deal with them. So don't be afraid to surprise yourself with your capacity and set this expectation high.

"I wish to show that age is no barrier. The word impossible is only in the mind and not in the heart. I lift these heavy weights to inspire people. When we, as human beings, are inspired, we do many good things for ourselves and also for the betterment of the world."

Sri Chinmoy after demonstrating how to lift an 8,000lb elephant, a 15-member human pyramid, a 2,229lbs car and Roberta Flack, as she performed a medly of her hits on a piano. He is founder of the World Harmony Run and believes that sports are a powerful instrument for promoting global harmony and understanding.

Challenge Profile

Trek Peru for Cancer Research UK

Maria Standen

Born 1974 – Product Manager for an European Bank

The Challenge - 65km trek across the Peruvian Andes

The challenge consists of a 65km trek across varied terrain and at different altitudes, which was considerably more challenging that anything I had taken on before.

On top of the physical challenge it was also a part of the world that I have always wanted to visit, with a culture that I find fascinating.

Cancer Research UK organised pre-trek weekends, mainly in the Peak District. These were invaluable in giving us an idea of the level of fitness required for the trek and it also gave people the opportunity to meet each other before the trip.

We raised the money and trained for the challenge as a team of 3, but approximately 40 people took part in Trek Peru. We were split into 3 groups for the daily trekking which worked really welll.

The support staff on the trek were amazing, as were our fellow trekkers who all had their own reasons for partaking in the Challenge. They all had a story to tell. It was an amazing experience.

The Charity - Cancer Research UK

Cancer Research UK is the world's leading charity dedicated to research on the causes, treatment and prevention of cancer.

I wanted to raise money for a charity which is close to my heart, having lost some family & friends to cancer and currently seeing my mother suffering with the disease for the 3rd time (this time it is terminal).

Between my husband, my sister and myself we raised over £11,500. This was done through a series of really successful events, like a big boat party on the Thames that raised £2,400, as well as some amazing generosity from family and friends.

We also undertook some presentations to help raise awareness of CRUK's work and why it is so important.

Fundraising Tip: Try and organise 'big events' and ensure that everyone is aware of what you are doing!

Diary

Best Moment

The best moment was reaching the Sun Gate on the Inca Trail on the final day of trekking and seeing Machu Picchu for the first time. Before going through the Sun Gate, we were congratulated and were awarded a medal by the staff. Very emotional!

Hardest Moment

The hardest day was trekking over a pass of 4,500 metres and for about 10 hours. We encountered a hail storm, heavy rain and a couple of the group needed medical treatment for altitude sickness.

Biggest Problem

With respect to fundraising before the challenge, the biggest problem was trying to explain to people that they were not giving donations towards a holiday for us! Another problem was that we had to approach the same people (family & friends) to support our fundraising events. It was also difficult fitting in the fundraising when working full-time. Our biggest mistake was thinking that it would be easy to raise £9,000 after the initial success of raising £2,400 at the Boat party! It got harder & harder. We were really pleased with the final total and in the end it was very rewarding to have made a contribution to such an important cause.

Training Tip: Wear in footwear by trekking in boots over varied terrain and for long periods of time, if possible on consecutive days at a weekend and carrying a rucksack simulating the day pack to be carried on the actual trek.

Maria Standen, celebrating the end of their trek at Macchu Pichu with husband Will on one arm and her sister Melanie Allen on the other.

The Options

You've established your capacity, so you are now better equipped to look at the options. The following are some of the most popular choices in charity challenges. They are only a few examples as ultimately the list of challenges on offer out there is enormous and those that you can devise are infinite.

Options for 1 day

You can achieve a lot in a day. Some of the world's single-day challenges are amongst the hardest physical tests on offer. Within a period of twenty-four hours you can push yourself to the edge of your limits and still be home in time for tea.

1 5-10km run, 20–40km cycle, Supersprint Triathlon (400m swim, 10km cycle, 2.5km run)

These are the most accessible challenges for people who, for whatever reason, feel that most physical tests are not within their reach. For many, the start of a 5/10km run or walk might represent the end of a very long road to basic fitness, to mobility or to recovery. Cycling may also be a more realistic means of completing a challenge for those who have suffered from injuries aggravated by impact.

▶▶ Race For Life - Over 500,000 women took part in 162 races across the country in 2005, raising millions of £s for Cancer Research UK.

▶▶ World Swim for Malaria - This event encourages indviduals and groups to organise their own sponsored swimming events, of any size and length. They aim to have over 1 million people swimming on and around the same day in December. This enables those of every ability to complete a swimming challenge.

2 Half marathon (13.1 miles), half century cycle (50 miles), Sprint Triathlon (750m swim, 20km bike, 5km run)

For a non-runner, a half marathon is a tough physical challenge that demands months of training. During a non-stop run or walk for between 90 minutes and three hours participants will have to rely upon a level of fitness that goes beyond normal 30 or 45 minute gym sessions done two or three times a week. Again, these cycling distances offer a rough equivalent to those unable or unwilling to undergo the potential stress that running can put on the body.

▶▶ Silverstone Half-Marathon - Almost 10,000 runners complete this flat and famous course of 13.15 miles.

▶▶ London to Brighton Cycle - Europe's biggest charity cycling event, with around 27,000 fundraisers pedalling approximately 58 miles from London's Clapham Common to the Brighton seafront.

3 Marathon (26.2 miles), century cycle (100 miles), Olympic Triathlon (1.5km swim, 40km bike, 10km run)

A marathon, 26.2 miles, is a seriously tough experience for any level of athlete, whether they are aiming to complete it within three hours or six. Dedication and commitment to physical conditioning over a period of at least six months is essential. For a total beginner, it may take more like eighteen months to prepare to run a marathon. In a personal sense, a marathon offers an opportunity to focus your efforts towards a very tangible and impressive goal.

London Marathon - The centrepiece of the UK charity challenge schedule, in which over 30,000 runners follow the streets of the capital for 26 miles amd 385 yards. By finishing it you will join a club of 572,000 worthy souls and add to the £250,000,000 raised through the event.

The Lyke Walk - Organised by Tall Stories, this tough 24 hour/67km walk takes participants from Osmotherley on the eastern side of the North Yorkshire National Park, to Ravenscar at the North Sea, across the tops of the North Yorkshire Moors.

London Triathlon - Supersprint: 400m Swim,10km Bike, 2.5km Run; Sprint: 750m Swim, 20km Bike, 5km Run; Olympic: 1.5km Swim, 40km Bike, 10km Run. A great course, exciting atmosphere and a chance to raise money for a charity of your choice.

4 Extreme Single Day Challenges

There is a range of extreme physical challenges in a variety of severe environments. These single-day endurance tests are some of the most intense experiences any professional athlete will experience. Such challenges offer incredible opportunities for personal rewards, team building and fundraising success, but you cannot take such tests lightly, as their extremities pose serious physical risks, from dehydration to hypothermia.

Mongolia Sunrise to Sunset 100km Ultramarathon – A beautiful but seriously tough Alpine ultramarathon around Hovsgol Lake near the northern border of Mongolia.

Ironman Triathlon – One of the most awesome tests of human endurance: swim 2.4 miles, cycle 112 miles and run a full marathon of 26.2 miles. The event takes the winners around 8 hours to complete with age group athletes potentially crossing the finish line for up to 17 hours.

L'Etape du Tour - For this tough mountain stages of the Tour de France, 7,000 cyclists come together in the Pyrenean town of Mourenx and ride the 110m course through to Pau in under 10 hours, with three significant climbs to encounter – Col d'Ichere, Col de Marie-Blanque and the 10 mile climb the Col d' Aubisque.

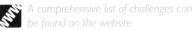

A comprehensive list of challenges can be found on the website.

2–7 day Options

There are 52 weekends every year and every one of them represents an occasion to take on some kind of physical challenge.

The step from one day to two or more increases the potential scope of your event. A hike could be extended to cover an entire range of mountains, or a single marathon could become a week of consecutive running challenges. Within a week, a huge number of major UK challenges can be completed on foot or on bicycle. This period of time therefore gives your project the tools to link and involve a huge number of places around the UK, and draw a lot of important attention to your cause. Over this same period you can also participate in some of the world's most extreme multi-day endurance events.

>> London to Paris Cycle – Run by lots of different charities and pitched at different levels, this normally consists of a 4-7 day trip, beginning and ending at famous city monuments.

>> Marathon des Sables – This 6 day, 151 mile endurance race across the Sahara Desert in Morocco has become increasingly popular with Brits in recent years, but remains and extraordinary and rare achievement.

>> Five to Seven Day Treks - There is a wide range of five to seven day treks on offer across famous and beautiful routes in countries such as Peru, Egypt, Vietnam, China and Nepal.

2 to 4 week Options

A commitment of more than a week gives you a chance to explore some of the most adventurous and challenging possibilities.

This kind of time frame presents the first real opportunity to go abroad. If your cause is a British one then the UK may well be the focus of your project, but if you aim to help an international charity, to link countries through different charities but similar causes, or to undertake overseas volunteer work, then start to think on a global scale. A number of single day and weekend endurance events take place abroad, but the two to four weeks category allows you to take on something more broad and substantial, in terms of distance and environment.

>> Raleigh International Borneo Multi-Challenge - Teams of four are dropped by helicopter in the Borneo Jungle, in Malaysia, where they have to build their own camp, run through paddy fields, cycle along jungle tracks and kayak into the South China Sea. They also abseil, white water raft and climb Kinabalu, the highest mountain in South-East Asia.

>> St Luke's Hospice JOGLE + 3 Challenge - An extreme endurance challenge combining 1000 miles of cycling with 24 miles of steep hiking. The challenge is to cycle from John O'Groats to Lands End via the UK's 3 highest peaks, completing the equivalent of cycling three-fifths of the Tour de France and climbing one-third of Mount Everest and in only 9 days.

3 to 12 months and beyond...

At this point your adventure becomes epic and your potential impact limitless.

Literally tens or hundreds of thousands of pounds can be raised and endless attention drawn to your cause. Fascinating awareness and adventure material can be produced, significant volunteering projects can be undertaken, massive distances can be covered and major human achievements realised by people of all abilities. The boundaries of what can be achieved within this period are those of your imagination and ambition.

LLoyd Scott on his way across Australia dressed as Sherlock Holmes

On May 4, 2005, at 0721hrs, the Commando Joe (Polar) team comprising Charlie Martell, Steve Clewley and Gary Bullen completed the Scott Dunn Polar Challenge in a record-breaking time of 9 days, 17 hours,39 minutes. This is the first of 3 extreme challenges that the Commando Joe team are set to undertake for the Meningitis Trust, in memory of a relative that died of the disease in 2003. In 2006, the team will compete in the inaugural Ocean Fours Rowing Challenge - 3,100 nautical miles, west to east across the North Atlantic. In 2007, it will take on the Marathon des Sables.

In October 2004, famous fundraiser and adventurer Lloyd Scott left Perth, Australia to cycle across the country to Sydney on a Penny Farthing in the guise of Sherlock Holmes. His remarkable journey took him across the Nullarbor Plain, down to Adelaide, across the Great Dividing Range towards Bondi Beach, Sydney, where he finished the 2,600 mile route in 3 months. He raised over £310,000 for Children with Leukaemia. Read more about Lloyd's feats for charity on page 117.

In 2004, Edwin Tucker completed a two-year round-the-world trip to raise awareness for the charity Practical Action. He circumnavigated the world by bicycle, using only renewable forms of energy (no planes, trains, buses or ships). When water crossings were necessary, human or sail power was used. In 2 and a half years he covered, 23 countries, 4 continents and 36,110km by bicycle and 2,000 nautical miles by boat.

Team and Corporate Challenges

If you are part of a team of any kind then you may feel that on top of the personal and charitable benefits of taking on a challenge, you would like to add a social or corporate benefit. As a team building exercise, charity challenges are second to none, bringing members together in an interdependent, testing and rewarding experience.

What can a charity challenge offer to all teams?

All teams rely upon teamwork, trust and mutual understanding. From the football pitch to the office, the individuals involved have to make personal sacrifices for the good of the group. A charity challenge provides a number of situations, including organisation, fundraising, training, preparation and the execution of the challenge itself, which call on these qualities.

What can a charity challenge offer to corporate teams?

Internal Benefits

- Takes team members out of the office environment and into new, stimulating situations.
- Acts as a bridge-builder within and between departments, which has a hugely positive effect on collaboration and communications issues.
- Gives team members a chance to demonstrate a variety of skills as well as develop new ones.
- Provides a challenging and original environment for team members to employ everyday skills in different ways, including planning, brainstorming, problem-solving, marketing, leadership, delegation and communication.
- Enables employees to build a better

relationship with their employer.
- Spreads a positive message around the company, particularly with the aid of internal newsletters and intranet resources.
- As a means of raising money towards an annual charity target or for a Charity of the Year partnership, such events are ideal.

External Benefits

- Corporate participation in a charity challenge adds to its reputation for community involvement and corporate social responsibility.
- Local media coverage of the event helps improve goodwill towards the company.
- Industry or sector press coverage improves the company's reputation.
- Challenges that are organised within industries or sectors provide ideal opportunities for developing business contacts and relationships.
- On donations made to charity in support of corporate challenges, the company can claim tax relief

"Challenge events build employee confidence and generate a tangible forum for teambuilding in a new environment. The fundraising element means that the whole organisation can back their team by getting involved."
Mike Bartlett, Head of the CARE Challenge Series

➤➤ In 2004 a team of Metro Inspection Services Ltd. employees organised a challenge themselves: to trek to Everest base camp for the charity ActionAid.

As we always do a major event each year for charity at Metro Inspection Services we decided that this could be the challenge for 2004.

We wanted to choose both an international and UK charity to benefit from the Trek. We chose ActionAid for our international charity but also stipulated that we wanted the donation to be specific to ActionAid Nepal.

For the team this was an absolutely spiritual and enlightening once in a lifetime experience. It was an honour to visit Nepal, a nation made up of beautiful countryside and amazing people, living in abject poverty but always able to smile and help you if required. It also really raised our awareness of the current civil problems with the Maoist insurgency in Nepal.

On top of the individual benefits and the satisfaction of raising so much money for charity, the challenge was a great builder of an extremely strong team, which has benefited us and the company ever since.

We felt that by organising the challenge ourselves we could keep costs to an absolute minimum and therefore maximise the amount of money we could raise for ActionAid. It also enabled us to visit the projects that we were helping. This really made a difference to see that everything we had been through over the course of 3-4 weeks of the Trek was really going to people who needed it most. It put a very real edge to the whole trip – what we did really could make a difference and we saw it first hand.

Tim Kitching, Metro Inspection Services

➤➤ Since 1996, FMC Technologies have entered CARE International corporate challenge events every year, raising over £50,000 for the charity.

In 1996 two of us at FMC were interested in entering a Three Peaks Challenge event for charity. The challenge of completing the three peaks in 24 hours appealed to us whilst raising £5,000 for international aid at the same time. This appeared to be an ideal opportunity for a good cause. We entered seven walkers and two drivers in one hired mini bus. We have gone back for more every year since!

Our team spirit is very high. On top of this there is great deal of personal satisfaction in completing the event and finishing high in the rankings, as well as knowing how important our annual contribution to CARE's work is.

It is an extremely effective team building event at very low cost. I have personally (with my team's help) organised FMC's team participation every year for 10 years. During this period we have had multi discipline and inter-departmental participation, even to the extent of having two different Norwegians from FMC's plant in Kongsberg for three of these years. Every team member, including the drivers, has thoroughly enjoyed each event and we now have a solid core for the team. There is also the potential to take part each year with completely new participants.

CARE runs well organised events with very high standards of safety and support during the event. The really personable and friendly CARE Challenge team members make a huge difference that we have known over the years.

Richard Preston, Team Leader, FMC Technologies

Challenge Profile:

'Mission Malawi' for ActionAid

Les Pratt

Born 1973 – Radio Producer

The Challenge - Lilongwe to Mzuzu by Bicycle

I was looking for a charity challenge, but none on the travel market seemed to satisfy my criteria, which were to raise money for HIV/AIDS relief and for that money to be spent in the country where the expedition was taking place. The challenge we devised was to ride 300 miles in 6 days from Lilongwe to Mzuzu. Having not been on a bike since I was 14, the sheer physical challenge of getting fit enough to cycle 300 miles in blistering heat was immense. By the time it came to leaving for Lilongwe, I had a team of 10 cyclists and two support crew members: a Zambian driver for the support vehicle, Godfrey, and a British tour guide, Stuart, provided by Discover Adventure.

The Charity - ActionAid

ActionAid are an international development agency whose aim is to fight poverty worldwide. They help over 13 million of the world's poorest and most disadvantaged people in 42 countries worldwide.

As a gay man, HIV/AIDS is something which confronts me every time I enter a bar or club, but the problem in Africa is running out of control, and no-one seems to take notice, despite the efforts of charities all over the world.

One morning, as I sat munching my cornflakes, I saw a BBC Breakfast report about the HIV crisis in Malawi and knew from that moment that I should do something constructive to help. We raised £40,000 for ActionAid and spent about £15,000 on the air fares, accomodation and equipment.

In the lead-up to the event, we visited schools in our area to talk to the students about what we were going to do and about the work of ActionAid and the problem of HIV/AIDS. Awareness of HIV/AIDS is pretty low and we wanted to play our part in addressing that. We also linked up with some of the HIV charities based in Manchester, who were very helpful.

Manchester's gay scene was our main focus for media coverage and we were able to raise some great awareness with their help. BBC Breakfast lent us a camera to film the expedition. The footage was used to make a 12 minute documentary as part of Commonwealth Film Festival in 2005

Diary

"To start something like this from scratch, convince 9 other people to participate and to raise over £40,000 collectively was a fantastic achievement that we are very proud of. It was an unforgettable experience and I can't wait for the next one!"

Best Moment

The best moment was just after we finished the ride. We were taken immediately to the ActionAid St. John's Project in Mzuzu, which was to benefit from some of the money that we had raised. Seeing a troupe of ladies doing a traditional dance in our name, and then meeting some of the orphans at the centre was almost too much to take in.

Hardest Moment

We'd spent the first two days on muddy forest tracks and the cool breeze that came off the mountains was a God-send. On day three, we reached the tarmac roads which skirted around Lake Malawi. The heat from above and below was unbelievable. On top of that, the distances on our schedule were completely wrong and we reached our final destination some two and a half hours after we'd anticipated. It wasn't a happy night!

Biggest Problem

The lack of cycling experience in the team meant that it took quite a while to get used to the bikes. we had three accidents on the first day, including Drew Stokes, who threw himself into a stream at high speed, David Warde, who launched himself headlong into a pile of loose chippings, and David Cawley, who toppled sideways in the mud and broke his elbow!

All smiles for the 'Mission Malawi' team as they reach Mzuzu and the end of their 300 mile cycle from Lilongwe.

Choice 2

Organised or Independent

Every challenge project is essentially independent. The responsibility for fundraising will always be upon your own back and the physical test will rely upon your own will and commitment. However, there is a fundamental choice to make if you have decided to challenge yourself for charity. Do you create, organise and complete a project independently or do you sign up to a challenge event or trip organised by a particular charity or a third party agent?

Make this decision for your own reasons and according to what kind of person you are and what you want from the project. Traditionally, independent trips have been taken on by an elite of more confident and experienced travellers and exercise connoisseurs. In fact they are within reach of anyone with the time and will. Similarly, organised overseas challenges have been frowned upon by some groups as physically pedestrian and too similar to an adventure holiday. In fact, operators can provide access to seriously tough and worthwhile challenges for anyone.

Organised

- Challenges that have been organised by a charity, operator or event organiser fall into this category and consist of anything from a 10km fun run to a two week overseas trek.

Independent

- Challenges that have been devised, planned and been undertaken independently by their participants, with only minor organisational support from their chosen charity.

Comparative Advantages

There is not a better or worse means of taking on a challenge for charity - there is just what is right for you. A look at the comparartive advantages of packaged or independently organised challenges will help you decide.

Achievement and Prestige

- Independently organising and completing a project gives you tremendous sense of achievement. The end product of thousands of pounds and increased awareness is totally a product of your own efforts.
- For those wanting to reach the very highest level of physical achievement, you may need the support and resources of organised events and expeditions.
- Justified or not, there is potentially less cynicism about independent projects than organised expeditions.
- Organised and annual challenge events offer them potential of recognised status and prestige, which will make fundraising easier: the London Marathon, the Marathon des Sables and the Ironman Triathlon to name just a few.

Choice and Control

- The central elements of the project – where you want to go, how far and by what means – are totally up to you and can be tailored to suit your own priorities and commitments.
- In a competitive market for organised package challenges there is a great deal of variety in destination, means and level of toughness.
- During the challenge itself you have total control over the pace, the schedule and the overall priorities of the project.

Your Cause

- There are far more opportunities to match the cause, the route and even the means, which makes for a far more effective project in terms of your impact on the chosen charity
- Volunteering projects and local community links are increasingly becoming part of the package offered by operators and charities. The experience and knowledge of the organisers will probably be greater than your own.
- On an international project, there is much greater scope for meaningful engagement with local communities through volunteering and project visits, as well as through everyday communication and friendships.

Safety and Support

- Going off the beaten track and taking on an extreme challenge in a foreign environment can involve many potential dangers and difficulties. A well-organised project removes these obstacles.
- With thorough preparation, accumulation and recruitment of skills and detailed risk assessments, independent challenges can measure up to the standard set by the best of the operators.
- Health and safety measures have to be meticulous. If you are concerned about your ability to complete the challenge due to health issues then this kind of back-up would be vital.

Personal

- As a team that has been through every stage of a project, from its initiation and early planning stages, through the fundraising and training process, to its ultimate completion, you will have developed a closeness and interdependence that is immensely rewarding.
- As a member of a large group or participant in a scale event, such as a marathon, you are able to experience the powerful mutual support, solidarity and excitement that add an incredibly rewarding element to the challenge.

Responsibility and Time

- All responsibility for the organisation of the challenge, from health and safety issues to scheduling and logistics, will be taken care of by others.
- If you delegate effectively and assemble a team of experienced participants and supporters then the complexities of a self-organised challenge will be simplified.

- There is an amazing range of organised single-day challenges for participants of every level of ambition.

Local Environment

- As an individual or small group your impact on local environments will be negligible, which can not always be said of some organised group challenge trips.
- Very high standards of responsible tourism are becoming increasingly common amongst charity challenge operators.

"Research shows that having the support of a group can be an effective way to achieve any goal, and can make a challenge more fun. Many of our members take part in charity fitness events and enjoy motivating and encouraging each other."

Christine Michael, Slimming World

A team of participants led by tour operator Charity Challenge reach the Uhuru Peak of Mt Kilimanjaro

"The medical support was a great encourage to me, especially Moyna - without her encouragement I would have found it much more stressful and may have given up. Diego was a good expedition leader, made decisions and gained the respect of all. The local guides are to be commended, their local knowledge and skills made for an

Dr Sean Hudson of Expedition Medicine, providing expert medical support for an ATD challenge in Nepal.

enjoyable time both at camp and trekking. Guides and support staff made an effective contribution to the success of our trek. I achieved my challenge because the Across the Divide team worked as a team. "

Desmond on his Northern Ireland Chest, Heart and Stroke Association trek to Patagonia with tour operator Across the Divide.

"Our project combined the physical challenge of cycling 80-100 miles a day with a fact finding mission about modern slavery in southern and eastern Africa. Anti-Slavery International set us up with their partner organisations across the continent, so every rest point involved interviews and research. This was the most rewarding

Rebecca Gowland waits for the rest of her team as they cross the Alps towards France (photo: Jonny Polomsky)

and exciting part of the trip and one that we couldn't have done without the freedom that being totally independent allowed."

Rebecca Gowland, on her independently organised Cape Town to London Cycle for Anti-Slavery International.

43

Choice 3

Choose Your Charity

This is the most important decision that you will make. Whatever your motivations are for taking on a challenge (and none of them are wrong) your choice of charity defines the entire experience. The physical challenge itself - its duration and toughness, your means and your preference for an independent or organised challenge, are all ultimately dominated by the raison d'etre of the whole project: the cause to which you are making a commitment of time, thought and sweat.

Every year thousands of marathons are run, overseas treks completed and miles cycled with only a passing thought for the affiliated charity. The charity, the participants and their sponsors are worse off for it. Thinking carefully about this and finding an issue that resonates with your conscience will make everything easier. By putting the work of a charity and your contribution to it at the front of your mind and connecting it to something at the bottom of your heart you will give yourself access to limitless determination and you will inspire those around you.

Sometimes making this connection is easy...

A Passion

If there is a cause you have always felt strongly about, something you have seen and thought: *"People need to know about this, this needs more attention"*, then it might just be a question of finding an organisation that addresses the issue in the right way and offers you the scope to get involved. Your enthusiasm and knowledge will set you up for making a real impact with your fundraising and awareness work.

Marina Khilkoff-Boulding with her disabled son Michael, who died in 1990. In 2003 she scaled Kilimanjaro in his memory and to raise money for Whizz-Kidz, who provide mobility equipment for disabled children. Read her profile on page 94.

A Person

Perhaps someone close to you has suffered or died from a disease or a condition which made you feel powerless. Expressing your feelings about this person by taking on a challenge in their name is both powerful and brave and inspires heartfelt support from sponsors. By providing a focus for others that were affected by this person, you have a pool of support and encouragement at your disposal.

A participant in Cancer Research UK's Race for Life dedicates her efforts to her parents

Challenge Profile:

Unicycling Across Britain for HOPE For Children

Rob Ambrose

Born 1980 – Teacher

The Challenge - Unicyle from Land's End to John O'Groats

This traditional route for charity cycle rides was an attractive challenge for a one wheeler! I decided to go for it after several friends had bet that I couldn't do it and another friend pointed out that there was a Guinness World Record on offer if I could do it in less than 14 days.

I learnt to ride a unicycle aged 14 and thought that if I could manage 10 miles, why not 900? It's unusual and fun and it was going to add an extra level of interest when it came to raising money and getting media interest.

I had a support team of 3. Jay drove his camper van. Paul and Steve took it in turns to ride a bike alongside me, so I always had someone to talk to and provide me with drinks as I went along. Jay and the team member not cycling would go ahead from town to town with collection buckets, phone local radio stations and newspapers, buy food and set up at each campsite.

I completed the challenge in 12 days 1 hour and 59 minutes, which was a new Guiness World Record.

The Charity - Hope For Children

HOPE for Children assist children, who suffer through being handicapped, orphaned, poor and exploited, in particular those living in developing countries.

Steve had spent his gap year in Zambia and we wanted the money to go towards helping some of the street children that he met whilst out there. Hope for Children run an education project for street children in an area of Zambia that Steve had spent some time in. We raised £4,500 for the charity.

We had lots of opportunities to talk to individuals, groups and to do radio and newspaper interviews in which we discussed what we were doing and why. We had also had a website, advertised on our t-shirts and support van, updated each day of the trip, which had lots of information and links; we also got front page articles in a couple of student and local newspapers, as well as a mention in The Sun and The Independent on Sunday.

Fundraising Tip:
Be determined and creative.

Diary

"Both the challenge and the charity were really imporatnt to me, which made finishing the unicycling and collecting the money immesnely rewarding. It is a feeling that I will never forget"

Best Moment

Day 10 was the best day for me. Having been reunited with Jay and a new support vehicle, I rode the stunningly beautiful 100 mile route from Glasgow to Fort William. Along the way we were met by a lovely young couple who had heard about the challenge on local radio in Edinburgh that morning and had driven out to meet us and donate some money.

Hardest Moment

On Day 6, tired and saddle sore after a very slow day of cycling we were just south of Preston when we heard that Jay had been in an accident.

Training Tip:
Little and often and build it up. In the weeks leading up to this challenge I rode 5 miles a day with a longer ride about once a week.

Thankfully he was fine but our support vehicle had been written off. This was a huge set back and we seriously considered giving up.

Biggest Problems

The accident presented us with our greatest problem. How would we carry on? In the end Jay went home with his van and returned with another vehicle. Meanwhile, Paul and Steve had to carry everything on bikes for 3 days. Organising the challenge itself was more work than I anticipated and as a result less energy was poured into fundraising than I wanted. In future, I would allow more time and get more people involved in organising this side of things.

Rob Ambrose and his team celebrat the end of their 900 mile unicycling challenge

Sometimes it takes more consideration...

The challenge itself

If your inspiration has come from a love of a particular sport or mode of travel, try to find a charitable cause to match. If you are a keen cyclist, you may relish the freedom and independence of cycling. Your choice of charity could reflect these passions by targeting an organisation that gives disabled people opportunities for increased mobility. Whizz-Kidz, for example, provides equipment for disabled children, and the charity Interadventure develops opportunities for disabled people to easily access the outdoors.

Your Community

Take a look around you. Within any local community there are problems that need attention. There are undoubtedly members that are marginalised because of disability, age, lack of opportunities, mental health or homelessness. Disabled people might need better access to facilities than local councils can provide, or the children's clinic might be lacking in a vital piece of equipment.

A Place

If you have travelled in the developing world, or indeed in many areas of the western world, then a particular place may have made a big impression on you and its social and economic needs affected you. Having already made an emotional attachment to the community finding a cause that you can identify with will be straightforward. This also gives you the advantage of using that place as part of your challenge.

Rhys gets mobile with a powered chair thanks to funds raised for Whizz-Kidz.

Unregistered and Private Causes There may be a certain individuals or groups that would benefit from your charity challenge support, however, they are not registered under the terms of the 1989 Charities Registration Act. This will cause a problem at many levels of fundraising. It may also be illegal. To comply with current UK legislation, you must only be raising money for a registered charity. This could simply be in the form of a trust fund for a friend who has suffered a serious accident, or it could be something much more substantial. Either way, always make sure that you are within the law before you begin.

Narrowing down the possibilities...

A charity is any organisation that provides a public benefit. In the UK alone there are over 180,000 registered with the Charity Commission (the charity regulatory body) and a further 220,000 unregistered but still considered part of the sector. Worldwide there are millions.

What Size of Charity?

When faced with such gigantic numbers the easy option is to simply head for the major brands. When you think about an issue there will probably be five or six large UK and international organisations that spring to mind. These charities have the biggest incomes, the greatest organisational and fundraising resources and also the widest scope of influence. From a negative perspective, they might be perceived as vast bureaucratic machines that swallow money with endless administrative costs, while failing to directly address the cause on the ground. On the other hand, as large and powerful organisations they may be regarded as the only charities that can make a profound difference to their target issues – issues that need attention on a scale that only the big guns can give. Then there are the little guys—the small charities that benefit enormously from the exposure your individual project provides.

Bigger charities (income of £10 million or more)

- Millions of £s invested in an increasingly well-known brand that is instantly recognised
- A larger pool of potential supporters who will have either direct or indirect experience of the issue
- A large supply of support, advice and fundraising resources, including a dedicated hotline
- Service centres all over UK, or even the world, creating potential stop-offs during your challenge and unlimited volunteering opportunities
- A means of contributing to a major domestic/global influence

Smaller charities

- A closer, more intimate relationship with the charity, its staff, its beneficiaries and its communities
- The potential for a large financial impact and tangible effect on the charity's work
- Normally lower administration costs and fewer objections to potential "waste"
- Scope for very valuable awareness work
- A smaller portfolio of corporate sector supporters, which will give *you* more companies to approach for sponsorship

What Type of Charity?

If there is a particular cause that you would like to support, but feel bewildered by the vast number of organisations addressing the issue, do not despair. This is a common problem for supporters of charities, from the average person on the street wanting to give a few pounds a month to trustees on the boards of multi-million pound international foundations. Ultimately, the answer can only be found in a combination of thorough research and your own beliefs. The main question is: what makes you feel comfortable and confident that your efforts are suitably directed? For example:

• Do you want an organisation that addresses the root or the result of the problem?

Cancer Research UK are dedicated to research on the causes, treatment and prevention of cancer.

Macmillan Cancer Relief is a charity that works to improve the quality of life for those living with cancer.

• Do you want to support an organisation that works internationally or concentrates on the issues domestically?

Shelter work to tackle the cause and consequences of homelessness in the UK, directly helping around 100,000 people a year.

Homeless International is a UK based charity that supports community-led housing and infrastructure related development in partnership with local partners around the world.

• Do you want your charity to enforce an ethical fundraising policy?

In May 2004, Nestlé offered £1,000,000 to the charity Breakthrough Breast Cancer. Nestlé suffer from negative publicity inspired by their extremely controversial approach to baby formula marketing in the Third World, which has been alleged to indirectly aid the spread of disease and provoke a rise in breast cancer (The Guardian, 6th May, 2004). By approaching a breast cancer charity, they were attempting to offset this publicity through positive brand association. Breakthrough, despite the benefits that an easy million would have reaped, said no.

There are a number of other questions that you feel will affect your decision as to what charity you pick. There is no right or wrong answer to these questions, but they are important for two reasons. Firstly, by researching them you will naturally find out more about the issue that concerns you. Secondly, having carefully considered this decision, you will have less reason to ever doubt it.

Much of this information can be found on the website of the organisation or within their annual review (any charity should be happy to send you a copy). If you want more details, phone and ask. If you are considering supporting a very small community charity—of which there are literally thousands—then ask to have a look at their constitution. It is important to know as much as possible about your charity so that you never have any doubt that what you are doing is important.

Your Chosen Charity

The relationship between you and your charity is a very important one, for both parties. Your challenge is only possible because they have enabled you to undertake it in their name, while their work reaps the financial benefits and publicity rewards. Although individual charities have different policies for defining the relationship between themselves and their challenge participants, there are a number of basic responsibilities and benefits within most.

What Your Charity Can Do For You

- Give you a reasonable level of support with your fundraising and training
- Provide you with as much information as you need about their work
- Answer any questions you have about fundraising law and practice
- Provide fundraising and awareness materials and resources
- Help organise, if appropriate, visits to their projects in the UK or abroad
- Offer lots of opportunities for you to continue your relationship with them beyond the challenge

What You Should Do For Your Charity

- Take full personal responsibility for the agreed fundraising target and your physical conditioning
- Represent them legally and professionally and sign any necessary fundraiser agreements with them to this end
- Ask them before using their logo on any new material
- Understand the details of their work and represent them enthusiastically and informatively

Independent Challenges

Independently organising and executing a challenge of your own design may seem like a win-win situation for your chosen charity – they get the money and none of the hassle. However, your project does represent some risks for them because it will be using their name. Having spent years developing the credibility and legitimacy of that name, they cannot afford to risk it being damaged by an independent fundraising project. So, when you approach the charity with your plans, which should be as detailed as possible, you should try and demonstrate the following:

- That you have the time, resources and experience to take full responsibility for the organisation of the challenge
- That you have the organisational skills and experience to minimise all health and safety risks during the challenge
- That the way in which you represent the brand of the charity is of the utmost importance to the project
- That you will refer to them for advice on the use and representation of their brand
- That you understand the legalities of fundraising and will abide by these as a priority
- That all the funds (after an agreed proportion of costs if this is necessary) will be paid directly to the charity

 Your project will not necessarily be part of a fundraising team's schedule for the year. This means that the support they provide you with is on top of all their other established commitments, so avoid being too demanding.

10 Ways To Get Noticed

Attracting attention is a major advantage for charity challenges – you have the chance to raise more money, generate vital awareness for your cause and amaze, amuse or astound onlookers.

1 Take on a Major Human Achievement

There are a few things left that have not been done before. Everest, rowing the Atlantic, swimming the Pacific, cycling the length and breadth of every continent have all gone, but there are more out there. To be a genuine physical pioneer you need serious training, resources and experience.

> On 10th May, 2005, as she reached the summit of Denali, Alaska, Annabelle Bond became the fastest woman in history to climb the highest peaks on seven continents, raising over £850,000 for the Eve Appeal.

2 Be the First

The first woman to swim the Pacific, the first teenager to reach the North Pole, the first Englishman to run around the world or the oldest person to walk from Land's End to John O'Groats. If so far it has only been tanned, buff American men, then now it's the turn of the British pensioner to take it on.

3 Put Together a Worthwhile Package

Organising a project that hopes to gain attention simply by creating a genuinely interesting and meaningful scheme could catch the public's imagination or not. A long, hard and unpredictable route could be coupled with extensive awareness work, a volunteering project and a topical and relevant cause.

4 Follow a Famous Route

There have been thousands of famous historical or mythical routes established, that have caught the imagination of the world for hundreds of years. Similarly, a map of the world is covered with important demarcations.

> In 1999, Alexandra Tolstoy and three friends travelled three thousand miles along the Silk Road through Central Asia and China. They became the first people to retrace this ancient trading route on horse and camel since the merchants of the Middle Ages and raised £30,000 for Merlin. (see page 160)

⑤ Choose an Emotive Cause

Some issues gain enormous amounts of coverage in the media. The cause that you feel strongly about may not have made a dent in the popular consciousness and you may rather address the imbalance and target an under funded crisis, but if you want to gain attention then you can become involved in a cause that is covering the front pages.

⑥ Be a Model Example

Charity challenges are a perfect opportunity to show people what's possible and what can be achieved. Most obviously, this is physical and psychological, but it can also be social, political, ethical or environmental: social inclusion, responsible tourism, ethical consumerism to name just a few examples. By making your project a model of best practice in a particular area you can attract worthwhile attention.

⑦ Give Yourself a Gimmick

The British mentality does not appreciate people who take themselves too seriously, but it does love those who are willing to do something ridiculous. Costumes and fancy dress are a perfect way of drawing attention to yourself. Making people coo in amazement at your bravery and at the same time chuckle at how ridiculous you look is a fantastic combination for raising extra money and awareness.

⑧ Take a Wacky Challenge

Hugh Sawyer is spending a year living in the woods around Oxford without a tent, whilst maintaining a city job in London and raising money for the Woodland Trust.

For a challenge to be worthwhile, it doesn't have to be an extreme physical test of endurance. It could also be a test of will in other ways, a sacrifice of lifestyle or a sustained period of discomfort. These imaginative and original angles make people smile and sit up and take notice.

⑨ Big Brother it

If the challenge is wacky enough and catches the popular imagination, you could approach a reality TV production company with a proposal for a programme. If you get a documentary deal in the pipeline then you have the opportunity to raise your profile with the media, the public and your potential sponsors. What happens to the ideals and purpose of your project, however, will no longer be in your hands.

⑩ Do It Naked

On the plus side, you are bound to get lots of coverage. Unfortunately, it is unlikely you will get very far without being arrested.

Challenge Profile:

London Marathon for Age Concern

Jennie Page

Born 1950 – Secretary

The Challenge - Complete the Flora London Marathon

In 1997 I underwent a life-saving operation, for the second time, to try and excise a head tumour. Although it was benign, the tumour can grow to such a size over a period of time that there is insufficient 'room' within the skull. I suffered complications during the operation (an artery was breached) leaving me paralysed down the right side of my body amongst other things. After intensive rehabilitation and physiotherapy over a two year period I was comparatively back on course. The tumour will, I know, re-occur in the future.

Independence is to be cherished and so I wanted another challenge after learning to walk and drive again and having got my life back together.

The London Marathon took me 6 days, 3 hours and 21 minutes to complete (according to the media!). My family, colleagues and friends were supportive for the duration. Over the six days, apart from the first day when I walked with a friend and colleague Mary Foulkes, my boyfriend, Rhodri Williams, never left my side. My family came up from Dorset for the final day and my mother, aged 82, walked the final mile and a half with me.

The Charity - Age Concern

Age Concern supports all people over 50 in the UK, ensuring that they get the most from life. They provide essential services such as day care, information and campaign on issues like age discrimination and pensions, and work to influence public opinion and government policy about older people.

I chose this because my brother, Anthony, works in the Dorchester branch as the co-ordinator for information and advice. A few years ago I received invaluable advice and support from Age Concern when my mother was ill.

I raised over £8,000 and through coverage from almost all of the national media, was able to raise some great awareness for Age Concern.

Fundraising Tip: Try and obtain as much sponsorship up front if possible – it will save a lot of problems later.

Diary

"I am not intending to participate in any further marathons – nothing will compare with the experience, elation of the one I have completed."

Best Moment

Turning into the Mall in front of Buckingham Palace to be greeted by the nation's press and television news in the company of my boyfriend, family and friends. It was very emotional. I was overwhelmed by the reception I received – I had no idea that it would cause so much interest. My main concern was that I wouldn't fall over in front of the cameras!

Hardest Moment

On the first day, with 33,000 people around me, I found it very daunting. Crowds, however 'friendly', and I are not compatible! After that experience with the exuberance and jostling of the crowds, I settled down to enjoy myself (if that's the right word!). It became easier as the days progressed.

Biggest Problem

in the days leading up to the start of the Marathon, I worried that I might not complete the course and

Training Tip: Perseverence coupled with determination!

let everyone down. However, I didn't have any real problems during the event, apart from a little lower back pain and a small blister.

Jennie outisde Number 10 Downing Street, having accepted an invitation to be a guest of the Prime Minister at the Queen's official birthday celebration on 11th June 2005.

Vehicle Challenges

A variation on these physical disciplines is to take on a challenge in a vehicle or on a motorbike. There is no doubt that these can be hard and gruelling, but in terms of the way a charity challenge represents a remarkable individual physical achievement, such trips don't quite fit the same criteria. However, this does not mean that a motor-powered project cannot be hugely inspirational and worthwhile, and there are many examples of this.

Some of the main ingredients from the ideal behind charity challenges will be lost, i.e. the physical test, but other ingredients can be added in much larger dollops to give motor based projects real value and credibility.

Awareness

With a motor behind you, you will have more time, range, energy and potential resources to raise awareness of your cause. Visits to schools, universities, associations and clubs can be done far more regularly and the tools that you can carry with you to do this can be much more sophisticated.

Interaction with the Cause

For many of the same reasons you will be able to shape your project around your charity and its work more effectively than slower and more cumbersome human powered challenges. You have the chance to link up hundreds of centres and thousands of people affected by an issue, an organisation or a movement.

Volunteering

To begin, end or intersperse your route with voluntary or charity work not only focuses its purpose but also gives you more legitimacy and undermines potential accusations of a motor holiday!

Recording the Trip

The ability to carry extra recording equipment and take more time to do such work gives you the chance to produce high quality and very powerful material. Such an asset sits perfectly alongside the extended involvement you can have with the cause and awareness work that you can undertake.

Top Tips

- Try and think of your trip first as an opportunity to achieve something remarkable through some of the above and base your entire project planning around this work.
- With this as the main emphasis, rather than simply a distance or route, you will be able to ask for sponsorship with more credibility.
- Cover all or most of your project's costs through your own resources or specific sponsorship.

Fundraising

Every charity challenge has to hit a fundraising target and whether you are raising £100 for a 5km run, £1,000 for a marathon or £50,000 for a year long trek, you need support. It is the most important, but also the hardest part of taking on a charity challenge and something that may seem a mystery to many. For years, participants have been raising money in the same way and making their job an unhappy and stressful one. Instead, fundraising for a charity and in the name of an amazing personal achievement should be an immensely rewarding process.

Out with the old…

- Constant worrying about hitting your fundraising target
- Ignoring the most important part of fundraising – a connection to the cause
- Nervously creeping round friends with a sponsorship form
- Relying upon a circular letter to your friends and family asking for cheques to be sent in
- A mountain of impersonal letters sent blindly to the FTSE 500
- Pestering the same people again and again
- Endless months of chasing up sponsorship money
- Forgotten thank yous and lack of recognition

And in with the new….

- Ambitious targets and great success in surpassing them
- Being passionate about your charity and using this to motivate yourself and inspire others
- Knowing the value of what you are doing and being confident
- Making it fun, easy and rewarding for people to sponsor you
- Putting on events and using a wide range of fundraising methods
- Getting people involved in different and interesting ways
- Understanding why people give and targeting the right audience
- Making supporters feel valued and encouraging long-term relationships with your charity

Why Do People Give

Giving money to charity is something that almost every member of the public and every organisation do regularly, whether it is 10p thrown into a tin or thousands of pounds donated every year. Every one of these decisions to give was probably different, but there are recurring themes to this generosity. Before you start looking for sponsorship and support it is vital to understand some of the motivations of those whom you are approaching. By knowing the main themes behind giving, you can tailor your approach and its style to those priorities.

Individuals

People give money as individuals primarily because they have been touched. They could be touched by sympathy and sadness for the plight of those you are helping, they

"We make a living by what we get, but we make a life by what we give."
Sir Winston Churchill

could be inspired by what you aim to achieve or they could be amused by your imaginative plans. Most people are by nature kind, supportive and generous when they are touched by something that they feel is worthwhile and, vitally, that they feel has the right impetus behind it.

Theories

This is the simple version. The complex one first looks at the emotional side of giving, such as the theory of Andreoni (1989), who divided charitable contributions into three categories of motivation:

1. **Public good theory**: people give if they perceive there to be benefits for their community as a whole or society as a whole

2. **Exchange theory**: people give to receive tangible benefits, such as recognition and improved social status.

3. **'Warm Glow'**: that the effect of giving on the individual inspires psychological benefits and provides a feel-good factor.

All of these are important for your fundraising work. When you start to create your product and devise your various approaches you should take into consideration what social benefits your project will give, how you can offer to publicly recognise supporters and how you will maximise their feel-good factor.

Next there have been very useful analyses of the age, gender and income of the individual. When beliefs, attitudes, past experience and knowledge are also examined the picture becomes even more complex (C. Walker, 2002). Ultimately the key conclusions that concern you from endless research into donor motivations are as follows:

Positive factors

- Giving increases with age, social class and income, however those from lower income families are proportionately more generous.
- Women give more than men and to more charities.
- People professing a religious faith often give more than those not.
- The concepts of empathy and sympathy are key: giving increases when the beneficiary is perceived to be similar or familiar to the donor.
- The greater the level of knowledge of the cause, the issue or the recipients, the greater the willingness to give.

- If people have given before to the same charity or towards a similar cause then they are more likely to give again.

Negative Factors

- A negative experience with a charity or with charities or giving in general makes people less likely to give again.
- Many people are put off by high (perceived or real) administrative costs.

It gets more and more difficult to get the chance to convince people of your worth every year. Charities that employ agents to pester passers-by on the street have turned high streets into a gauntlet of awkward excuses and fake phone calls. They are also contributing significantly to the development of a knee jerk "no" culture when it comes to charity. People do not want to explain their desire not to give and why should they?

Large Corporations

These organisations are regarded by most independent fundraising projects as an enormous source of charitable funds. Not only do they appear to have mountains of spare cash lying around, but they also seem to be involved in charitable partnerships wherever you look, whether it is through cause-related marketing on a product in the supermarket or the sponsorship of a charity event. This, unfortunately, is a myth. Corporate giving over the last twenty years has become considerably more focussed upon tangible benefits.

Now companies undertake relationships with charities or causes for three main reasons:

- To strengthen their reputation locally, nationally and internationally
- To generate goodwill towards their business or their brand
- To engage their employees

This is achieved through a far more focussed set of relationships. These can be divided into those that are exclusive to charity organisations and not independent challenge fundraising projects and those that offer some opportunities.

Opportunities exclusive to charity organisations

Charity of the Year

A company chooses, normally through a staff vote, to support the same charity for a year. The advantage of this is that rather than having a minimal effect on lots of charities the company can achieve something substantial and tangible for a single organisation.

Cause Related Marketing

CRM is the use of a charity brand and a charitable donation as another means of swaying consumers to choosing a certain product.

Corporate Foundations

A certain percentage of profits is channelled into a fund, from which money is distributed according to strict criteria that are usually centred upon a) the communities surrounding the company's major operations b) a cause that relates to the product or the consumers that it targets. These foundations very, very rarely give to individuals.

Give As You Earn

Companies often give a lot of their cash donations as an extension of their employees' contributions to charity through their payroll. This improves employee relations by rewarding their generosity and maximising its impact.

Volunteering

This is a very current trend. By supporting their staff organisationally, financially or simply by allowing them time out of the office to volunteer within the community, companies can substantially improve their internal relations as well as the public's perception of them.

Opportunities for charity challenge fundraisers

Matched Giving

This is the most profitable and the easiest means of getting support from large companies, if, of course, you work for them. As part of their efforts to marry charitable giving with employee relations, companies often match the money that the individual has raised (often just within the firm) up to a certain amount.

Gifts in Kind

Out of all of the large corporate methods of giving to good causes this is the one that offers the greatest hope for independent challenge fundraising projects. Gift in Kind donations are given as a product or a service. For example MFI provides furniture to good causes and BT provides communications training and advice. You need equipment and services for every aspect of your project – specialist equipment, publicity materials and every element of a fundraising event to name just a few.

Sponsorship and Advertising

Big sponsorship deals are the holy grail of challenge fundraising trips and although the competition is fierce they are out there if you sell yourself in the right way. How exactly to package yourself and approach companies is dealt with in detail in sections of this chapter.

Ethical Fundraising

The issue of what donations or partnerships should be refused on ethical grounds is a controversial one. The economy is rife with exploitation and unethical investment but at the same time, money from this economy keeps charities *going. So where do you draw the line? The only answer is to establish for your project what sources of funding you do not want to attract and so do not spend time soliciting them. It would be hypocritical to accept money from an organisation that directly or indirectly perpetuates the problem that your charity is working to address, or even issues that surround that problem. Some would take* *it further and strike off any company with a bad reputation for blatant exploitation and environmental or ethical negligence in any field. The key issue is what the impact on your project and your charity of associating with a particular brand or organisation would be. Consult your charity if you have any doubts or questions about this.*

Small & Medium sized Companies

Smaller businesses are a far more suitable target for the company fundraising that your project undertakes. This is because businesses without large corporate structures rarely have strict guidelines for charitable involvement, they rarely have a focussed agenda for the type of goodwill such involvement should generate and they rarely have corporate social responsibility or community affairs departments.

When decisions about donations, sponsorship and advertising are made by the individuals at the top of the company in a relatively ad hoc fashion then you have considerably more scope to influence them. In huge companies, stringent criteria normally always guide decisions and these criteria will normally always exclude you. Individuals in small and medium sized companies are often guided by their own priorities, feelings and experience. Consequently, concepts that apply to the motivations of individual donors also apply here.

Within local communities the people who run businesses are often only too happy to get involved with a local project, simply because they want to give something back. Some of the other reasons why small/medium sized businesses make contributions to charities are as follows:

- To generate goodwill in their community, which will often make up the vast majority of their consumer base
- To tap into new local opportunities for business, such as clubs, schools or other local organisations
- To advertise cheaply and constructively

When you imagine fundraising from businesses your first thoughts will probably be huge brands such as Nike, BP, Virgin and Barclays. These companies receive thousands of applications for funding for independent fundraising projects and send out an almost equal number of rejections. Think small and local first then work your way up as you gain momentum and confidence.

Organisations and Association

Charity committees within schools, clubs, Rotary or Lions clubs, universities, church groups and unions, among others, normally always have a budget for charitable giving. They also have the resources to raise money specifically for you.

The potential interest in your project comes from personal connections between members of the group and members of the organisations. The relevance could come from any number of angles. Anti-Slavery International, for example, in their fight against human trafficking, work to defend fundamental employment rights, much as employee unions do. A project in support of this cause would therefore have an immediate relevance to many unions.

Similarly, breast cancer charities have a relevance to women's groups, disability mobility to sport's clubs and faith-based projects to religious groups.

Local organisations and associations will provide important support and also offer you ideal opportunities to raise awareness amongst all sorts of social and cultural groups. Some to think about: the Rotary Club, Women's Institute, Round Table, Freemasons, Lions Club.

Grant-Giving Bodies

Trusts and foundations, are predominantly set up for a specific purpose, such as providing educational support for underprivileged children, supplying resources for arts projects or funding for heritage sites.

Similarly, they have sometimes been established in the aftermath of a tragedy or in memory of someone or something, such as Cancer Research UK's Bobby Moore Fund; and therefore they relate to the consequences or prevention of these tragedies. Most of these kinds of Trust and Foundations state clearly that they do not consider applications from individuals. Furthermore, those who support the work of your charity, would rather receive an application directly from them and may already have.

Other grant-giving bodies that are set up as part of an organisation or association, such as a school or university, are far more likely to consider applications requesting support for independent projects. This will be particularly true if the project includes

a close relationship with the cause and includes volunteering and awareness work. These grant giving bodies usually target specific groups of people, such as:

- Students at a particular institution
- Members of a particular organisation or association
- Those of a particular age
- Those living in a particular area
- Those working in particular professions
- Those belonging to a particular faith group.

Trusts and Foundations are a vital source of income for most charities so make sure that you check with them first if you are planning to make an application for funding.

Why might people NOT give to charity challenges?

Some people just don't give money to charity, while others may feel that they already support enough and do not have the resources to contribute to your cause. However, there are also those who may have objections to sponsoring a charity challenge. This is linked to all the issues raised in 'Why?', but most often focuses on the costs of challenges and how these are being met within the project. The best way to deal with these objections is to meet them head on and remove any doubts within the minds of those you are approaching, whether they be individuals, companies or other groups and bodies.

Covering Your Costs

For many challenge projects there will ultimately be three choices concerning the issue of costs:

1. That you should not be asking people to cover your costs, so every penny of expenditure will be covered separately.

2. That you will contribute as much as you can afford towards the cost of the project, and use sponsorship to cover the rest.

3. That your contribution of time, effort and determination is sufficient, so the costs can be covered totally from money raised.

The answer to this will come from the charity's stipulations, your own resources and your own attitude. Most charities realise that some of those taking on challenge fundraisers will not be able to cover all, or indeed any, of the expenses themselves and this will be reflected in their guidelines.

However, it gives you a distinct advantage as a fundraiser if you can tell people that their donations will go straight to charity. It undermines their immediate reservations and also gives you more credibility and prestige. If this is an advantage that you want then there are two ways of approaching it:

1. To use your own money or borrow money to cover the costs.
This is an impressive and worthy approach, which adds another string to your project's bow: on top of your sacrifice of time and effort, you are also willing to commit money to what you feel strongly about.

2. To raise money for your expenses separately to the charitable funds.
By collecting donations directly towards the costs of the project from sources who are happy to provide this kind of support, you are able to approach more reticent sponsors unhindered by the cost factor. This will improve your chances of raising more than your initial fundraising target. These are the sources most suitable for that:

• Family and close friends, to whom you will be able to explain in more detail the necessity of these costs and your overall fundraising plan.
• Corporate sponsors whose donation of money or gifts in kind are not charitable but in return for PR benefits

Whatever you choose to do, make it absolutely clear exactly where all the money raised is going and why. Never leave yourself open to accusations of misleading sponsors, which will negatively affect your chosen charity.

Fundraising 1

Sponsorship and Support

Getting money, help, advice and time through the garnering of sponsorship and support is the main aim of your project. This section guides you through a thorough and rewarding method of making the most of your fundraising potential. Fundraising is traditionally just the soliciting of money. However, a charity challenge does not just need money, it needs all kinds of support to make it successful and effective. Therefore you need to see fundraising as the gathering of as much support as possible, in whatever form.

NEEDS, RESOURCES, PRODUCT, APPROACH

Getting money and support from people can be tough and there is no room for dithering and fretting. With time, thought and the right process you will surpass your target with ease. Approach this challenge as you would any problem and methodically break down the job in hand:

1. NEEDS: What do you need?

2. RESOURCES: Where are you going to get them from?

3. PRODUCT: What are you going to use to get it?

4. APPROACH: How are you going to get it?

1. NEEDS

The first job of the fundraising process is to write a list of what you need. This will grow and develop alongside your fundraising and training, but it should encompass as many of the aspects of your project as possible.

- **Money** - your fundraising target; donations towards expenses
- **Other Sponsorship** - equipment (fitness, specialist, clothes, camping, safety, health, communications, recording (video, photo, audio)); flights/travel
- **Services** - printing; postage; IT; design; telephone; fax; internet; photocopying
- **Exposure and Awareness** - media (local, national, international – press, radio, television); audiences (clubs, schools, universities, unions, churches); website; documentary; publisher; PR (contacts, materials)
- **Events** - venues; guests; raffle and auction prizes; music; food; drink; decorations; entertainment; advertising; sponsorship; volunteers and committee
- **Advice and Support** - fundraising and training; voluntary sector; routes; places to stay; safety; expeditionary; health; political; financial; logistical; technical (specialist equipment, camera, mechanics); a treasurer; general time and support for fundraising
- **Route contacts** - people to stay with; support; equipment; health; food

A perfect fundraising role model - Flora Frank (left), 61, has raised over £120,000 for Norwood having run 11 marathons: 9 London Marathons and 2 New York Marathons. In 2004 she won the Jewish News Community Hero award for her fundraising efforts on behalf of Norwood, who have provided her brother Nissim Moses with specialist residential care for over 40 years. She is pictured here with fellow fundraiser Jane Jeffe.

London Marathon – target £3,000

Money: £1,000 in charity donations – friends and relatives; office colleagues; company charity coordinator for matched giving; local clubs and associations
Sponsorship: discounted trainers

Services: logo design; website design; small scale printing/photocopying of fundraising resources

Exposure and Awareness: local radio and newspaper contact; local school contact

Events: pub for regular quiz (£500); venue with all licences for party; DJ/band; food and drink suppliers; raffle/auction prizes and promises; sponsor for event costs(£1,500)

Advice and Support: training partner; medical advice; volunteers; general time and support for fundraising

⟫ London to Siberia Cycle – target £30,000

Money: £15,000 in sponsorship; £5,000 to costs; friends and relatives; high net worth individuals; college RAG committee; local clubs and associations; relevant grant giving bodies; Russian and international route related businesses, organisations and associations

Sponsorship: international corporate brand for costs; cycling equipment; specialist clothing; return flights; video and photography equipment; medical equipment

Services: website design and maintenance; logo and graphic design for presentation; large scale printing/photocopying; high postage costs;

Exposure and Awareness: UK and relevant international media; relevant local and national schools and universities; international schools and universities along route; UK production companies; UK and international cycling press and clubs

Events: three different venues for 2 x 300+ parties(£4,000 each), fashion show(£4,000) and concert(£2,000); event organiser; large number of volunteers; food and drink suppliers; Russian brands, businesses, organisations, associations and entertainers for Russian-themed event; fashion industry; bands/DJs; lighting, PA and presentation equipment; raffle and auction prizes and promises; office fundraising team (£1,000)

Advice and Support: route advice, accommodation and support; webmaster; expedition advice; road cycling safety advice; general time and support for fundraising.

2. RESOURCES

Having established what you need, you must now establish where you are going to get it from. Explore every angle and possibility.

Your Own Resources

Before you look elsewhere, establish exactly what resources you yourself have for your fundraising.

- What facilities do you have access to?
- What are your relevant skills and experience?
- What useful materials do you have?
- How much money can you commit to the project?
- How much time can you commit?

People

Now you can expand the circle as far as possible, filling in all the gaps that your own resources have left out. Everyone you know, and indeed everyone they know, offers one more opportunity for support. Before you charge in and send letters asking for money, think carefully about how best to involve people, bearing in mind that the people can offer support in different ways. Think as broadly as possible, because everyone can offer some kind of support. Time, for example, is hugely valuable in the fundraising process and something that you may be short of. Ask yourself the following questions:

- What they do and where do they work?
- What time do they have to help you?
- What resources do they have access to?
- Do they belong to any organisations, associations or clubs?
- Are they going to be able to support you financially?

- If so, at what level and what is the best means of approaching them?
- If not, how else could they offer support?
- What interests them and what would make them feel valued?

This list will be the basis for your fundraising approaches, but don't feel as if this has to be definitive. The rule is that you must have a relationship with the potential funder or supporter. If you have none or if you run out, then you need to develop more.

Networking

This is a horrible word and one that conjures up images of superficial socialites flirting their way around cocktail parties. However, if securing support is about developing a relationship with a potential donor, then you have to put yourself in positions to meet such people. Remember, what you aim to achieve is worthwhile and constructive. This means that you should feel confident about telling people about it, but at the same time avoiding coming across as self-righteous. The more people that you make aware of what you are doing and what help you need, the more likely you are to receive support. Another part of the networking process is plugging yourself into existing, relevant networks. For example, there may be a local business network or partnership that you can approach as a community, with shared interests and priorities. Clubs and associations are often networked together for mutual benefits. Once you have found a source of support then there is no reason why you cannot ask if they belong to a special interest network, or if they know of similar sources that might be willing to consider an approach.

Other Relevant Groups

To take full advantage of the contacts that you have, and to develop new ones, you need to consider what audiences will be interested in your project. If, for example, the local community sits at the centre of your cause and your challenge, then this is where the greatest focus should be. If any other aspect of the project seems to lend itself to receiving attention from a particular group of people, then this lead needs research and planning. Look at the challenge, its route, the cause, the means, your local community and the members of the team if you are in one, including their race, religion, social background and occupation.

When you start to lose motivation, draw on your initial motivations and focus on the positive impact that the money will have. Remember that you are going to put yourself through a remarkable physical challenge that demonstrates your commitment to a cause and illustrates its importance. This extract from Tony Clayson's Kilimanjaro Trek diaries is a perfect example of this dedication.

We had been advised that it took 5-6 hours to reach Gilmans Point, the top of this path, and having set off at about 11.30pm we knew that this increasingly difficult toil was to continue all night. I can without doubt say that the next 6 hours were the hardest of my life as I felt increasingly tired and unable to move. At times I would relax with my breathing and find myself becoming unsteady on my feet staggering about due to lack of oxygen. I learnt this could be corrected by increasing my breathing consciously. As we ascended people started to become ill and had to be taken down. Some were vomiting, others staggering uncontrollably and one girl just collapsed. Ray and I continued although afterwards both admitted we had felt in the worse condition of our lives.

On at least three occasions I felt I could go no further but each time drew on the love, support and encouragement I had received from home to keep me going. I was also driven by the desire to reach the summit and in so doing heighten awareness of Whizz-Kidz, a charity whose work providing mobility for disabled children was very close to my heart. This constant physical and emotional battle continued non-stop for 6 hours without any relent and was very taxing. The path then changed from a scree trail to a difficult rock scramble which sapped energy levels further. This too seemed to go on forever until somebody said there was Gilmans Point only 50 yards above. This lifted our spirits but that last 50 yards seemed to take forever with arms and legs moving at a snail's pace. The elation of reaching the summit was indescribable...

Without doubt this is the best thing I have ever done with my life. It has changed my life completely and inspired me to want to undertake a further challenge for the same cause in the future.

3. YOUR PRODUCT

The key to successful fundraising is to first develop and then take best advantage of as wide a circle of contacts as possible. The further this circle widens from you, the harder it is to ask for support and the harder you have to work. You are asking people to buy into what you are doing and therefore you need a product. The more attractive this is, the more people will support you. Impress everybody, value everybody and instead of this circle widening further away from you it will close in, making more and more potential support accessible.

You may be able to get a certain amount of support by making people feel obliged to give, but your potential as a fundraiser is multiplied infinitely if you can make people WANT to give. This is what a great product can do.

To take advantage of all this potential you have to make an impression. For a challenge fundraiser the impression will be formed on the back of the immediate hit of the prospective achievement: *"Wow! That's amazing!"* Secondly, the cause must have an impact: *"It's an important charity and its great that you feel strongly about it"*. This will be influenced by factors partly beyond your control, as they may well already have an opinion on your chosen charity. Thirdly, your imaginative and creative way of combining the two should strike them: *"I've been approached before, but this is original and interesting, and I like that."* Finally, you will sway them with your attitude, your persistence and the style of your approach: *"They haven't just written me a circular letter and they have made my support seem important and valuable."*

Your Product's Assets

What does your fundraising proposal have going for it and what is going to prevent it from slipping into obscurity alongside the thousands of other projects that are taking place? You have to attract people to your project from many different angles, inspiring as many emotions as possible.

1. The Achievement

Give your challenge a particular edge by making it more focussed:

- Distance - of particular importance or relevance
- Target completion time/period – personal best, particular time/position, records
- Extreme – what makes your challenge harder than others?
- Fundraising target – related to the challenge in general; related to your performance; a special achievement for yourself or the charity
- A package of challenges – is this event part of a longer term effort to support an important charity?

Challenge Profile:

Burnside River Expedition

Ed Bassett

Born 1959 – Lecturer in Expedition Skills and Land Navigation

The Challenge - Source to Sea open canoe trek on the Burnside River, Canada

I wanted to carry out a true wilderness journey for the challenge, so we plotted a tough route over the the the length of the Burnside River in Arctic Canada from Lupin Mine on Contwoyto lake to the settlement of Bathurst Inlet on the Arctic Ocean in the Territory of Nunavut. This represented a real challenge due to the remoteness, difficulty and location of the river.

We used a 17ft Open Canoe, an Old Town Tripper, which is the traditional craft used by indigenous peoples and European explorers. The other team member was Surech Paul, whom I have done a lot of expeditions with and we are great friends as well as experienced paddlers and adventurers. We are both members of the Royal Geographic Society.

The route was 240 miles and we completed it in 16 days.

The Charity - Heart of Kent Hospice, Maidstone

The Heart of Kent Hospice, and hospices across the country, provide essential palliative care for people with life threatening diseases as well as support for their families.

However, these hopsices are not funded centrally or by NHS Trusts. They rely on donations, fundraising events and legacies to provide their services, free of charge, to patients.

Through the expedition we not only wanted to raise immediate funds, but also to create a platform for its long-term sustainability and draw attention to the need of hospices across the UK. We worked closely with the local community and with local media and businesses to create new sources of funding.

The £10,000 we raised was a great help to the Heart of Kent Hospice and in addition to this the main sponsor of the project set up a charitable trust that supports children's charities in Kent.

Fundraising Tip: Although the donation that you make from the challenge is important, you should also work to inspire long-term relationships between your supporters and your charity, which can help them sustain their work for years to come.

Diary

Best Moment

Coming face to face with a male arctic wolf while eating our dinner on the riverside. He had obviously never seen a human before and seemed curious. No threat just curiosity! The moment lasted a couple of minutes but will stay in my memory forever.

Hardest Moment

The hardest period of the expedition was "portaging" (carrying our boat and equipment along the shore due to impassable waters) for 4 miles on rough terrain.

Biggest Problem

Throughout the whole expedition the mosquitoes and black flies were a constant source of annoyance.

"The Burnside River expedition was a very personal project for me. When my father died I really felt the need to do something as a homage to him, something that would make him proud. He was ill for nine years and if there had been a hospice near our family home some of his suffering could have been alleviated. I felt that supporting my local hospice would be a good way of letting him know that I loved him even if I hadn't taken the time to tell him while he was alive."

Training Tip: Don't over train and allow adequate rest periods between workouts.

Ed Bassett and Suresh Paul are flown in to begin begin their remarkable river journey by canoe

➤ Jane Tomlinson was diagnosed with breast cancer when she was just 26 years old. A tumour in Jane's lung grew so large that it made her breathless. Then in August 2000 a scan revealed multiple secondary cancers. Jane's diagnosis was terminal. But through a series of amazing challenges Jane has raised over £1,000, 000 for her four chosen charities and proved to others who are touched by cancer that life goes on and anything is possible. Her challenges have included the 2002 Great North Run in Newcastle; the London Marathon in April 2002; a John O'Groats to Land's End cycle on a tandem with her brother Luke Goward; the Ironman UK Triathlon in August 2003 and in June 2004, Jane and her brother completed a mammoth 2000 mile, five-week tandem bike ride from Rome to Leeds.

2. Fun and Creativity

Draw attention to your challenge and make people interested and entertained:

- Fancy Dress – entertaining, brave and brilliant for raising awareness
- Route – a particular start and end point or famous/relevant route
- Means – an imaginative or whacky way of getting from A to B
- Extra challenge – something you have done to make the challenge harder

➤ Jeffrey Archer's £1 per inch marathon challenge. One thing that can be said confidently about Jeffrey Archer is that he knows how to raise money. In 2004 he undertook to break the sponsorship record for the London Marathon by raising over £1,661,220. This sum works out as £1 per inch of the 26 miles and 385 yards, which is how the project sold itself: supporters would sponsor a number of inches or metres, making their contribution more tangible and interesting. Archer broke the previous record.

➤ Brothers Steve and Pete Fleming kicked a football for 250 miles across Malawi from the national stadium in the capital to ActionAid's St. John's HIV/AIDS project in the northern city of Mzuzu to raise £10,000 for the charity, as well as raise awarness of the issues in the UK and demonstrate the role that football can play in tacking AIDS. Walking through the country would have caused a stir, but kicking a football sent people into a frenzy of excitement! The project gained international media coverage and established positive links with local and national football organisations in the UK ad Malawi.

3. Benefits and Positive Consequences

What will result from your project? Who will benefit and how? Every positive outcome of your challenge is another asset.

For **Your Charity**
- How much of the money you raise will go to the charity?
- Exactly what will the overall sum achieve?
- Exactly what will a donation (of various sizes) achieve?
- How many people will be affected and in what way?
- How much awareness will you be raising and amongst what groups?
- How does the charity benefit from such exposure, and what is unique about the awareness that you can raise?

For **Social Awareness of the Cause**
Your project can inspire others to find out more about the cause make it more significant within the popular conscience. If the charity is Amnesty

Paul Parry gained extra attention on his way from A to B by picking up volunteers on his tandem. Here he gets a boost from Miss Universe, Jennifer Hawkins. Read a profile of his challenge on page 84.

International Challenges

Ideally, your cause and your route should be intertwined within the project. This bring direct benefits to your host environment. However, there may be many good reasons why it is more suitable to take on a challenge abroad for a domestic charity. If this is the case you must consider the impact of your project upon its host environment/s, just as a scientific or geographical expedition must do the same. Consider the ecological, environmental, social, historical potential of your project, as well as any aspect that might contribute to a better understanding of the world.

If your challenge takes you to a developing country, you can enable people to become better acquainted with the area generally. If this is the case then how are you going to communicate this new knowledge? Demonstrate this broader benefit through a clear schedule of presentations, articles and papers.

International, for example, how will you contribute to public awareness of human rights abuses?

For Yourself

It may seem strange to try and attract support by detailing the benefits of your project to yourself. However, remember that ultimately people give to people. It is human nature to support those that you feel an affinity with. Furthermore, if you are open about the benefits that you or your group will receive, then potential supporters will be less cynical about your motives than if such a question is left unaddressed.

If the cause has a particular personal resonance, then be open about it. The emotion that inspired the project, whether it is grief, sadness, frustration, joy or fascination, is important in itself.

• Does the project represent a positive personal landmark? Are you embarking on a voluntary undertaking for the first time? How important to you is "giving something back"?

- What will be the positive impact of the challenge on you as a person?
- How will you benefit from a greater understanding of the charity, the cause or the route?

"In 2003 I completed the Race For Life after months of training and preparation. My aims included losing a lot of weight and in doing this I gained lots more support and even some coverage from local newspapers and national magazines."

Claire Clark, 34, after completing the 5km Cancer Research UK **Race for life** in Cardiff alongside 10,000 other women

For **Other Fundraisers**
If you believe that such projects are socially valuable and you have conveyed this about your own project you can also help others realise their ambitions. This is a worthwhile repercussion of your challenge and one that can be aimed at community groups.

"In 2001 I heard Miles Hilton-Barber speak on his expeditions and was inspired by his bravery and by the thousands of pounds he had raised for the RNIB. If a blind man could show this courage, then I had to do something myself and since then I've raised £35,000 for three chairites by completing 6 different challenges."

David Brown, 44, having completed a 10km fun run, a half marathon, 3 marathons and an overseas trek in Egypt.

Independent Challenges
If you are planning your own challenge then individuals, companies and any grant giving body, organisation, association or institution will want reassurance that your project is:

- Legal and legitimate
- Safe and risk-assessed
- Well organised and planned

Legal and Legitimate
The most obvious way is to ally early on with your charity and ask them for a supply of headed paper, a letter from an employee or trustee sanctioning and supporting what you are doing and a range of promotional material. It also helps to gain the endorsement of people in respected positions and from organisations and institutions. For example, if you are a school or university group then get an endorsement letter from a teacher, headmaster or tutor; if your charity has a well known patron, ask the charity if they will consider signing a letter for you.

Safe and Risk Assessed
Go through the process on page 199-200 and demonstrate the results of this concisely and clearly in any application.

Well organised and planned
Any application document should include details of who is going and what their relevant experience and qualifications are. This aspect should also be demonstrated in all communication with potential sponsors.

4. Potential Rewards

Apart from laying out clearly the positive outcomes, you also need to be able to offer recognition and rewards for those supporting you, where appropriate.

Individuals

Having had a good look at the kind of factors that influence individual donors, you now need to compile a list of potential rewards that you can offer them. The kinds of recognition that tend to attract individual donors are as follows:

- A list of donors on the project website and in project literature (event programmes, summary documents etc)
- Different levels of recognition within these resources for different levels of donation
- Sponsorship of a particular element of the project. Just as construction projects offer to inscribe bricks with the names of donors, so an inch, a metre, a mile, a leg, a region or a country could be offered as a means of making a prospective donation more tangible
- Link donations to specific elements of the charity's work. This could be a piece of equipment at a special needs school, or the provision of help for a certain number of refugees for a certain period of time.
- Newsletters, photos, updates or a CD/DVD of the challenge
- Membership of the charity's supporters or special benefactors group. If you are asking for donations to go specifically to the charity then you can work with them to design benefit packages for sponsors

Companies

For all types of sponsorship/support:
- Positive exposure in magazines and newspapers
- Tailor-made updates and articles for use in internal literature and external PR
- Website links and details of potential impact
- Recognition of support and details of potential impact
- Supply of some promotional materials to illustrate involvement (photographs, DVD)
- Multi-media presentation to employees on completion

For equipment sponsorship:
- High quality photographs of their equipment being used in exciting or extreme conditions
- Detailed product reviews in as many environments as possible
- Articles and features in industry/specialist press

For event sponsorship:
- Tailor made exposure within relevant consumer groups
- Distribution of promotional materials at the event

Grant-giving bodies

- Monitoring and updating whenever and however required
- High quality photographs for use in the promotion of the body's work
- Multimedia presentations to groups within the body's sphere of influence

Bringing Everything Together: **Documents**

You have accumulated a range of information about the impact, the benefits and the legitimacy of your project, which can best be used to attract support of all kinds. This information needs pulling together in a Summary Document.

Whatever the scale of your challenge this is a very useful document to have – it can be enclosed with a letter, attached to an e-mail and used as a basis for all your requests for fundraising and as a means of attracting interest and support from all sorts of people. I have used the two-page model as a guideline, not a rule. Two pages provide enough space to summarise the majority of projects and to give any information additional to that included in the cover letter about the support you are asking for. Furthermore, at the stage that this document is sent out, the potential supporter will not require more information than can be comfortably provided in two pages.

Two-Page Summary Document

To include:
• The overall aim of your challenge
• A summary of the work of your charity/cause
• The benefits and consequences of the project
• The rewards of involvement
• Details of the challenge and the physical achievement
• A brief review of the participant/s
• If necessary: a timeline for the project, a budget and a risk assessment

Lay out:
• Head the document with the logo of the charity and the project
• Foot the document with the charity number
• Avoid blocks of text – use bullet points when appropriate
• Break the document into clearly headed sections
• Use pictures, maps and diagrams where possible
• Do not use less than a point 12 text

Project Folder

This document constitutes an expansion of the two-pager and is great for those undertaking larger scale challenges who are looking to attract big donations or sponsorship deals and therefore have to provide more information about the project. You can split the folder into more detailed sections, such as the *Route*, which describes why you chose this route, what you know about it, what the benefits and dangers of travelling through these areas are and how much you plan to cover everyday. The *Budget* section is particularly important, as this is your chance to demonstrate that you have considered every source of income and every likely item of expenditure, and that these two sides are realistically balanced.

Just because it is more thorough does not mean that it should be any more difficult to read, so follow the same guidelines as above. Make your project folder interesting, imaginative and professional. It should contain everything that a potential supporter might want to know, as well as being enjoyable and inspiring to read.

2. THE APPROACH

You know what you need to make your challenge successful, rewarding and profitable and you know where to get it. You also have all the tools you need to solicit support. Now you have to go out and get it.

Golden rules of The Approach

- Avoid at all costs writing to someone that you have not spoken to or e-mailed or who is not expecting to receive something from you.
- NEVER write to "Sir", "Madam" or "whom it may concern".
- Be passionate, professional and knowledgeable
- Be specific about what you want, without being demanding or expectant
- Be explicit about EXACTLY where the money is going

Establishing your Contacts: Categories

The people that you are going to approach for support fall into two main categories and this will dictate the way in which you first approach them:

➤➤ **Category 1** - Once removed from you: friends, family, colleagues, close contacts, i.e. this is anyone with whom you have a friendly and immediate relationship

➤➤ **Category 2** - More than once removed from you: if the main link to this person is through someone else then they fall into this category

Go through your list of contacts and place a 1 or a 2 next to them. The number of contacts that fall into the first category should remain constant, while those in the second should multiply as you exploit your immediate circle to its full.

Developing your Contacts: From Category 2 to Category 1

Your job as a successful fundraiser is to draw more and more people into Category 1. Remember, fundraising is based upon relationships and if you don't have them then they need building though contact development, research and initial communication.

Contact Development

- You need to develop your relationship with Category 2 contacts as far as possible. This might involve meeting up with them, telephoning them, e-mailing them
- Get in touch with the intermediary contact, i.e. the Category 1 contact that links you to this potential supporter. Ask if they can mention to the potential supporter that you will be in touch with them and tell them something about your project.
- If you have a contact at an organisation then they will need to give you the details of the person or department within the organisation dealing with Community Affairs/ Charity/Sponsorship and Advertising.

Research

If you are seeking support from institutions, organisations or high-profile individuals then you need to do some research. The internet is obviously the place to start for this kind of work and most companies and grant giving bodies will have on-line resources. For smaller organisations and individuals you want to find out as much as you can without being in the least devious. Be open with friends and contacts, explain that you are trying to find the best way of approaching and would like to find out some background information.

What do you need to know?

- **Individuals:** Would the cause have a particularly controversial, emotive or personal meaning? Do they have a trust that deals with their charitable giving? Are they linked to other organisations or groups?
- **Companies:** What is their policy on charitable involvement? What are their guidelines? What exactly does the company do? What markets do they aim their product at? Are there previous examples of the company's successful support of challenge projects?
- **Organisations/Associations:**
  What is the common factor of their membership? What are their main purposes and activities? What is the decision-making process for this kind of support?
- **Grant giving bodies:** What exactly are the criteria for grant applications? What is the guiding purpose and ethic of the body? What are some other examples of projects that they have supported?

Initial Communication

The first golden rule must be applied here: avoid at all costs writing to someone you have not spoken to or e-mailed or who is not expecting to receive something from you. Even those you know well will respond better to a request for support if they know it is coming and have some background information straight from you. For total strangers, making a successful "cold call" is a difficult thing to do, particularly at the corporate level, when you will probably be speaking to someone who wants to get rid of you as soon as possible, normally by telling you that they "*do not do this kind of thing.*" The key is to try and engage the person and get them interested in you and your project as soon as possible. Be charming, courteous, friendly, and direct as well as efficient with their time.

Telephone calls

- Know exactly who you want to talk to. Avoid asking for "the person that deals with…" This will mark you out as an unsolicited call immediately
- If you are phoning someone you do not know, then mention your mutual contact straight away if you have one. Make clear the influence of this person in recommending that you call
- Briefly describe the most relevant and interesting aspects of your project
- Do not expect an answer then, but instead ask if you can send more information about the project and what involvement you are looking for and/or ask if you can meet them (for those you want more substantial support from).

E-mail

- An e-mail performs the same function as a phone call for people who cannot, or do not want to be reached by phone, so follow the same guidelines as above.
- Make e-mails brief, courteous and relevant to the recipient.
- Ask if there is a convenient time for you to call to discuss the project, or if you could arrange a brief meeting at some stage.

 Every communication you have with a potential supporter will leave an impression on them, so throughout you should come across as passionate and professional about what your project will achieve.

The Ask

Everything is in place and you have all the relationships and tools you need for the final push. Here you need to make sure that you avoid these very common mistakes:

- Coming across as impersonal - no-one wants to feel like they are one of a thousand recipients of the same ask.
- Asking everyone for the same thing - money is not necessarily the most valuable thing that some potential supporters can offer the project.
- Expecting the relationship to end with a donation – this should be the beginning of their attachment to the project and the cause.

Letters and E-mails

The drafting of a good fundraising request is an art, but one that anyone can master. The key is to imagine each recipient reading the letter or e-mail and ask yourself what might put them off, what might they not respond well to and what will make them cynical about your motives or unenthusiastic about the project and the cause. Keep the main body of the letter or e-mail short and succinct, and always enclose with it your project summary document or for really ambitious requests, a copy of the project folder.

Tone and Style

There are two main approaches to writing fundraising letters. The first is to write an essentially serious letter, explaining the toughness of the challenge, the value of your project and the cause, as well as the needs of the charity. These letters are aiming to impress people with your commitment and guts, capitalise on the individual's sense of social responsibility and inspire empathy with the charity's benficiaries.

The second is to go for the more entertaining approach: *"Guess what I'm going to do? Yes, that's right, I'm mad, but it'll be worth it!"* These letters are much lighter, with a serious note encompassed to demonstrate the worth of the project, but essentially concentrating on your challenge and their sense of adventure and fun. A combination of the two is also an option.

Structure

Introduction

- Refer to your link to them or your last contact with them
- Explain briefly what you are doing and what support you are looking for
- For a company, organisation or grant-giving body, lay out the relevance of your project to their priorities or criteria

First Paragraph

- Personal and emotive reasons which have inspired you to take the challenge and what the physical achievement will represent
- A brief summary of what your cause does, how you will contribute to it and what this means to you

Second/Third Paragraphs

- More details of what your challenge consists of
- Details of what support you are looking for
- What impact different levels of support will have
- Any potential recognition or incentive that is attached to the donation
- How simple it will be for them to support you.

Sign Off

- As you should never be writing to strangers (unless specifically asked to) this will always be *"Yours sincerely"* or something more informal for friends and family
- *"Yours faithfully"* is used when you have written to an unnamed recipient – *"Dear Sir or Madam"*.

Trimmings

- The letter should be written on your charity's headed paper to which a logo relating to your particular project can be added – at their discretion
- Make sure it is obvious where people should reply to, particularly if the letter has two sets of contact details: yours and those of your charity

What to Include:

- Enthusiasm and emotion that will engage people
- Logical arguments as to the importance of your project and the money and awareness you aim to raise
- Real life examples and human interest stories
- Plenty of opportunities for people to find out more information
- Having prompted action, give simple and efficient means of taking it

What to Avoid:

- Insincerity or arrogance - both are a massive turn-off to potential supporters
- Assuming too much knowledge about the work of your charity - people do not want to be confused
- Jargon - use simple language that is accessible to all
- Vast reams of text - break up your letter into easy to swallow chunks

Mr J. P. Smith
72, Warminster Road
London
SW11 3TG

5th January 2006

Dear Mr Smith

Thank you very much for your time on the phone yesterday and for giving me the opportunity to write to you. I understand that my uncle, Peter Clark, has told you something about my fundraising project. I aim to raise £30,000 for Save the Children and awareness of the ways in which the HIV/AIDS crisis in sub-Saharan Africa has tragically affected millions of children. On 25th July 2006, I will set out from Dar es Salaam in Tanzania to walk over 4,000 miles to Cape Town, South Africa, unsupported and unaided. I would like to ask you to consider supporting my efforts with a donation.

In 1999, during my GAP year, I worked in a remote rural school in Botswana teaching English. Its community was being devastated by HIV/AIDS and in my village alone, 25% of children had been orphaned by the virus. I am passionate about the need for more attention and more resources from the UK to be mobilised for this cause. Save the Children works to prevent HIV/AIDS and support children who are affected by it and £40,000 will help this charity continue and develop this crucial work.

For every 1 mile I walk I need to raise £10 in sponsorship. I would like to ask you to put your name to a portion of my challenge. I not only want to inspire people to support me financially, but also to draw their attention to the crisis. Even if you cannot help me with a donation, I would like to ask you to read the two enclosed leaflets and to sign-up to my e-mail updates.

I have attached a summary of the project and would be happy to send you a full project folder should you wish to get more involved. I need support in so many ways and yours would be hugely appreciated. Also enclosed is a freepost envelope and donation form if you wish to sponsor me. Alternatively, visit my website, www.AfricanWalk.com.

Many thanks for your time and consideration

Yours sincerely

James Brown

Challenge Profile

A to B for British Red Cross and Victim Support

Paul Parry

Born 1979 – Writer

The Challenge – Cycling 6,000 miles from the Scandinavian town of A to the Nebraskan town of Bee

I was considering a route for a charity fundraising cycle for some time, but wanted to do something original. I said to a friend: "*I need a reason to go from A to B*" when I remembered a Trivial Pursuit question of "*where in Scandinavia is the town of A*". So I would start in Norway in A. But where was B? 2 weeks later we found the closest on offer: Bee, in Nebraska USA.

A month later, whilst planning the route, my brother commented rather cynically "sure, cycle 6000 miles - why don't you do it on a tandem and pick up hitchhikers". He walked off, I wrote it down.

The route covered 5600 miles, across Norway, Sweden, Denmark, Germany, Netherlands, Belgium, UK, USA, Canada, and back into the USA. A tandem made me stand out, and the back seat allowed me to be joined frequently by local volunteers. I completed the distance in 4 months.

The Charities - British Red Cross and Victim Support

The British Red Cross is a leading member of the largest independent humanitarian organisation in the world - the International Red Cross and Red Crescent Movement - providing relief to people in crisis, both in the UK and overseas.

Victim Support helps people affected by crime, providing free and confidential support to help you deal with your experience.

First I decided on Victim Support who I was volunteering with at the time ,then I added the Red Cross when the plans developed into a more extended international trip. I also raised various funds for the American Red Cross. I have raised £15,000 for these charities and because of the originality of the idea I attracted lots of media attention, which raised vital awareness.

Fundraising Tip: Get more people involved and give them defined roles and let them take some ownership of the mission. It is all too easy to get lost in all the organisation and lose momentum for the fundraising

Diary

"From the moment I thought of the idea of cycling from A to B to the moment I finished, it has been the most exciting and rewarding thing that I have ever done."

Best Moment

Riding into Bee, joined by 30 other cyclists, being given the key to the city and being made honorary Chief of Police of Bee! Meeting Miss Universe and giving her a lift on my bike was pretty good too! (see a photo on page 75)

Hardest Moment

I was almost arrested on a Canadian motorway, when I missed some signs and ended up stuck in a one-lane enclosed 10 mile section of road. I didn't want to stop or turn around as I'd been going for 8 hours and needed to get to Montreal. I had to climb over a wall with the tandem and cycle on gravel for 8 miles, and was then taken off the motorway by a Canadian police officer who spoke no English.

Biggest Problems

Any day spent cycling in Norway was tough - no one cycles there and they have bad roads, big mountains, and huge distances between towns. Next would be the American hitchhiker who really didn't pull his weight or the worst sun tan in history: brown arms and legs from just above the knee, white everywhere else – and worse still: a more tanned left-side after cycling thousands of miles Westwards!

Training Tip: For cycling, grab an exercise bike and then you can train in a gym/at home whilst reading and researching your trip, or simply watching TV. And you're less likely to get knocked off your bike!

Paul Parry marks the start of his journey from Å to B.

Maximising Your Success

1. Get the Most out of Sponsorship Requests

This is your main opportunity to make people WANT to be part of what you are doing, so pull out all the stops and be confident. On top of this there are a few ways of making sure you are getting as much support as possible:

- Ascertain exactly what the best kind of support they can offer is, or give them an option of supporting you in a number of different ways – through a donation, a ticket to an event or a prize for a raffle for example.
- Give a variety of imaginative options for financial sponsorship, linked to some of the angles that you have used, such as your time to complete the challenge or your impact on the charity
- Make the request individual and personal and use your special relationship with them as the basis for support
- If you only have time to write group e-mails, then divide your contacts into relevant sections – work colleagues, school friends, club members etc. Addressing these people as groups with a shared connection to you and each other will give them a shared interest in supporting you.

2. Make Giving Easy

Hassle-free giving is essential. Many potential supporters will have the money and the inclination to make a donation, but neither the time nor the commitment to go out of their way to do so. If they can donate in one minute then they are not going to be put off.

- Include a link to a donations page, where money can be quickly and efficiently pledged, in letters and e-mails
- Include a tear-off or printable donation form which sponsors can complete in seconds
- Include a self-addressed and preferably stamped envelope. Your charity may also be able to provide you with freepost envelopes.

 An increasingly popular and successful way of gathering sponsorship is through fundraising pages on specialist websites such as justgiving.com or bemycharity.com. There is more information about the avaiable options on page 118.

3. Chasing Up

Although your challenge is hugely important to you, it is a long way down the list of priorities for the majority of people that you are approaching for support. This does not mean that they might not become interested, but it does mean that t you will have to push it back into their radar as often as possible.

The key to following up a request for support is to remind without pestering. So, when you follow up a letter or application, strike a balance between being too demanding and being overly apologetic. At this stage you are at a significant advantage if you have been in regular touch with the individual before the "ask" was sent and if you have made efforts to develop a relationship.

Sponsorship Forms

A huge number of charity challenge participants use sponsorship forms provided by their charity to collect promises of donations and details of their supporters. Although internet sponsorship pages can be quicker and more efficient, they are not always appropriate and the traditional means may suit your fundraising approach. To get the most out of your sponsorship form consider the following ideas:

Maximising Donations
- Keep the form with you ALL the time, as well as a pen and a small resealable bag to collect donations.
- Photocopy your form and ask family and friends to collect sponsorship for you. Ask them to read these tips!
- Target groups of people - in the office, the pub or your sports club. This will also help with collecting their donations.
- Consider linking donations to a particular aspect of the challenge, such as the completion time or distance covered.
- Explain to people how important their

"The first person on your sponsorship form sets the level that everyone will follow, so make sure that you ask someone generous to sponsor you first!"

Kate Stocken, PR and Sponsorship Manager, Cancer Research UK's Race for Life

donation is while they are filling in the form.
- Make sure that your sponsor fills in the necessary Gift Aid details and ticks the box (see page 90 for more information).

Collecting Sponsorship
- If sponsorship is not linked to any aspect of the challenge then collect as many of the donations as possible up-front. Aim to collect at least half of the money before the challenge.
- When you collect their details, note down a date and place for when you will see them next.
- Ask them how they would like to make their donation - via a fundraising page, by post or in person.
- Make sure that you can read their contact details - thousands of pounds are lost to uncollected donations and this is a common problem.
- Follow up your sponsors straight after the event, while the blisters are still fresh! They will soon forget about their promise and you will lose motivation.
- Let them know how important their donation is when you follow them up. Once they have sponsored you they have made a commitment that they have a responsibility to fulfil it.

Team Fundraising

All fundraisers should try and assemble a team of people to help them, but if you are taking on a challenge as a team then this job is done for you – just make sure that it becomes a help rather than a hindrance.

All Teams

Establish a team target and individual targets

If the total target for a team of 10 participants is £20,000 then decide how much your combined efforts will raise and how much each individual should bring in. You should aim to surpass the target, so create a competitive but positive atmosphere, with an incentive for the most successful fundraiser.

Put together a plan

The team target needs breaking down into pieces. Putting on events as a team is great fun, rewarding and profitable, so be ambitious with an array of events. Look at resources that the group as a whole have access to. This will probably be related to the body which has brought you together.

Divide up the jobs

Everyone has different skills and they should be taken advantage of. At the very least you will need a team leader/ co-ordinator, a treasurer, someone to liaise with the charity, and each event will need an event manager and assistant.

Hold regular meetings

Keep a check on progress, discuss and share fundraising ideas and prevent individual members from falling behind at group meetings. Make these positive and encouraging – bickering within the team will only get worse as the challenge approaches. Also try and train together as often as is possible – if you are taking the challenge as a team, then vastly different levels of fitness will prove a big problem.

Corporate Teams

As page 36 shows, corporate challenges can be hugely beneficial to a company. The main principles of fundraising still apply and the methods described above remain the same. However, there are a number of techniques that work particularly well in a corporate environment, and some particular opportunities that you need to take advantage of.

Involve the Company/ Management

The company management needs to be involved from the very start, not only as they can offer vital support, but if you are representing their organisation you need permission to do so. Be clear about all the benefits (page 36) when you are selling the idea and be specific about what support you want and what impact it will have. Some of the opportunities:

- The company may have a pound (£) for pound matched giving scheme
- Sponsorship of fundraising events or

of the challenge itself
- A tax deductible donation from the company to your charity
- Private donations from management
- Use of company resources and facilities for your fundraising work – printing and photocopying, office supplies, food and drinks, meeting rooms and cafeterias.

Draft a Business Plan

In an office environment where problem solving, planning and executing schemes is the meat and veg of your daily existence, approach the task in hand in exactly the same way.

Spread the Word

If your team spans a number of different departments then you have a headstart in getting the rest of the company involved in the project.

- Find willing work colleagues around the firm to act as champions – ask them to become involved on an event committee, collect sponsorship or support your efforts in some way
- Use newsletters, notice boards and the company intranet to tell people about what you are doing and advertise your fundraising initiatives
- Don't forget how important awareness of your cause is to your charity – particularly in the corporate world. You may be responsible for the start of a much larger and profitable relationship between the two.

Between 2003 and 2005, 66 year old Bryan Kennett, a long term employee of Tesco Head Office, completed the Bike the Nile and Trek Peru challenges for Age Concern. The support he received from Tesco was amazing and this became part of a relationship between the two organisations that ultimately resulted in a lucrative Charity of the Year partnership in 2005.

"Piggyback"

Once people know about your challenge and fundraising efforts it will be easier to take advantage of existing opportunities.

- Find out about the social and charitable initiatives with the firm and discuss how your project could fit in.
- Find details of the various events calendars in the company and try "piggy-backing" as often as possible

"If you are intimidated by what seems like a huge fundraising target then don't worry! Approach in the same way as you would any office project: look at what resources and facilities you have available; put together a business plan; break up the jobs into manageable parts and delegate them around the team."

Tanja Knierim, Fundraising Officer, CARE International.

Involve Suppliers and Clients

Mobilise business partnerships and take advantage of goodwill to call in favours. Measure your request by the nature of the relationship and remember that gifts in kind or services may often be far more appropriate and forthcoming than financial donations.

Gift Aid

What is it?

Gift Aid is a government scheme that allows charities to reclaim the tax that has already been paid on donations made by individuals (not companies).

How does it work?

- After a Gift Aid declaration form has been filled in and the donation made, charities then reclaim the money from the government. If you pay a higher rate of tax you can claim further tax relief in your Self Assessment return.
- The donor must be a UK tax payer and the amount claimed by the charity must be at least equal to amount of Income Tax and/or Capital Gains Tax that the donor pays.
- The declaration can be applied to all donations made since 6th April 2000 and to all made in the future, until the declaration is cancelled. If the donor stops paying Income Tax or Capital Gains Tax then they must notify the charity when making another donation.

 Gift Aid only applies to donations made directly to a registered charity.

Sponsorship

- Each donor must fill in separate Gift Aid forms for each donation – you cannot simply accumulate sponsorship then make a donation yourself using Gift Aid.
- Sponsorship from people "connected" to you (a relative or in-law) cannot be made as Gift Aid donations.

The Question of "Benefits"

- The donation must be a gift – it cannot be received in return for a "benefit", such as a dinner ticket, an auction prize or a chance to win in a raffle or lottery.
- BUT – the Inland Revenue allow a small benefit to be received in return for a donation. This is mainly designed to allow for benefits such as discounts and membership schemes, although there is some allowance in charity auctions.

 Link to Inland Revenue pages giving all details

Your Charity

- If you have any doubts about what you can or cannot do then contact your charity or the Inland Revenue.

The Form

- Most charities will have a form that you can use for sponsors to fill in, so ask your charity first.

If you have to do your own, or get the declaration made as part of another document, then you need to include the following:

- Full name, title, home address (inc. postcode) and amount donated (£)
- A tick box or signature and date, alongside a declaration which says something to the effect of: "I would like all my donations made to the charity **** since 4th February 2002 and all donations made henceforth until I notify them otherwise to be treated as Gift Aid donations."
- Include a tick box asking if supporters would prefer not to be contacted in the future by the charity.

Fundraising Accounting

For any size of challenge you need to be organised and accountable when it comes to finances, for your own peace of mind, the accounts of the charity and its reputation.

Sponsorship Record

Keeping a good record of the fundraising process is very important and can be done very simply on a computer or in a notebook by creating a **fundraising spreadsheet**. It should consist of a breakdown of all your income and expenditure in as much detail as is necessary for your project.

 Download a template for your fundraising spreadsheet

The detail and thoroughness of your expenditure budget will depend upon the scale of your project. However, the accounting of the sponsorship you receive and the accuracy of the fundraising spreadsheet are crucial.

Every donation that comes in must be entered as soon as possible on the spreadsheet. If you are receiving cheques at home or at work, then this is simple, but there will always be occasions when you cannot enter the information straight away. So you need a process that every member of the group sticks to. Here are some tips for dealing with lots of sponsorship money coming in a variety of ways:

- You and anyone regularly involved in collecting sponsorship should carry around a small resealable bag with a sponsorship form, which has Gift Aid details on it. Any donation goes in the bag and the donor fills in a Gift Aid form. You know where it came

from, you have 28% more if they pay tax and they feel confident that their money will not be spent in the pub later on.

- If there are a number of fundraisers or team members everyone should have a copy of the Fundraising Spreadsheet to record donations made to them and then one member is appointed Treasurer and/or all the information can be e-mailed or communicated to the Treasurer who is responsible for the collation of all financial details on the main spreadsheet.
- Start a bank account for the project, with permission from your charity

Bank Accounts

Opening a bank account for the project is advisable. However, to get the most out of the money that you receive it should only really be used for (a) money received specifically for expenditure which therefore cannot benefit from Gift Aid and (b) your own contributions and expenditure. When you are selling tickets for events, auctioning prizes at a dinner or receiving money as part of a specific corporate sponsorship deal, then your charity will not be able to claim the tax back. The people paying for these things will also be much more comfortable making out cheques to a neutral account rather than individuals. As most events will also demand expenditure, then you will need to be able to draw money to pay for these and for it to be accountable.

For the actual challenge, if it is one that demands group based expenditure, then a bank account will be an essential part of your finances and their accountability. Expedition accounting is dealt with in detail later on in this chapter.

Fundraising Codes of Practice

As soon as you sign up to a charity challenge event or make a commitment to take one on for a particular charity, you become a fundraiser and therefore governed by a number of laws (covered in full on page 93) and obliged to follow certain codes of practice. Don't be intimidated by these, but do make sure that you understand them. As you are working essentially as a volunteer for a particular charity and using their registered charity number to legitimise your efforts, they ultimately have responsibility for you, so if you ever have any doubts or concerns, contact them.

Your Status

There are three possibilities to describe your role as a fundraiser within the law and The Institute of Fundraising's Codes of Practice:

1. **A volunteer fundraiser working 'in aid of' a charity** – you have no authority to act in the name of the charity and will be raising money for that organisation in your own capacity.
2. **A volunteer fundraiser working 'on behalf of' a charity** – you become an agent of that organisation which will be responsible for your fundraising activities.
3. **A professional fundraiser** – you are receiving a "clear and more than notional" benefit…which is, or might be, more than £500".

There is a huge grey area here, so it is important to establish at the outset exactly what your status is with your charity organisation. It is their responsibility and in their interests to lay out exactly what the terms of the relationship is. If you have any questions about anything you are doing then ask straight away – their reputation is the most important factor.

Your Responsibilities

Although these need to be established by your charity, you basically have two main responsibilities regardless of your status:

- To comply with all UK laws which relate to fundraising activities
- To represent your charity with integrity and with their reputation and best interests in mind.

Fundraising Legalities

All Fundraising

- Use the registered charity number on everything you produce for the project: tickets, posters, sponsorship forms, letters, t-shirts.

Sponsorship and Donations

- All requests for donations to charity must be done with an attached registered charity number.
- All funds raised by you for the charity must only be received by this charity organisation.
- Any personal information collected about donors or supporters must only be used only in compliance with the Data Protection Act 1998.
- When a proportion of the money raised is being used to cover costs, or a part thereof, then this must be made clear to donors.

Collections

- Obtain a Street Collection License from the relevant local authority (the council or metropolitan borough) for all collections in public (a place where the public have unrestricted access to all the time). These are limited and need applying for well in advance (min. 1 month)
- Get permission from the owner or manager of private property (e.g. shopping centre manager, station master)
- Obtain a House to House Collection License from your local authority for collections that move from place to place. For business premises, such as pubs, you also need the permission of the owner or manager.
- During all collections, you must wear ID badges and use sealed collection tins.
- All collectors must be over 16.

Events

- If the venue where you are holding an event does not have a licence to sell alcoholic drinks then you need to apply for an Occasional Permission from the local police. Similarly, if you wish to offer alcohol as a prize for raffles and auctions then you need an Occasional Permission. However, it is legal to sell tickets that can then be exchanged for an alcoholic drink.
- Food safety laws apply when you are selling food.
- There should be a trained and qualified First Aider present.

Raffles and Lotteries

- If you want to hold a raffle at a one-off event, like a dinner or party, you are selling tickets solely at the event, you do not spend over £250 on prizes (donated prizes do not count) and there are no money prizes (vouchers do not count) then this counts as a Small Lottery, for which you do not need a license. The result of the raffle must also be drawn at the event.
- Any lottery or raffle other than those described above need a Lotteries License from your local council or metropolitan borough. Liability for the legal organisation of a lottery falls onto the person/persons promoting it.

Challenge Profile:

Kilimanjaro Trek for Whizz-Kidz

Marina Khilkoff-Boulding

Born 1949 – Property Lawyer

The Challenge - Reach the 5895m summit of Mt. Kilimanjaro, Tanzania

 My disabled son, Michael, died thirteen years ago and before he passed away I used to say "If he dies I'll climb Kilimanjaro!" but I never did and fell back into the humdrum of life until Whizz Kidz gave me the chance to do it.

The Kilimanjaro challenge takes 10 days and involved 9 months training. The group was made up of 34 participants, all raising money for Whizz-Kidz, 8 guides, 103 porters and the whole Whizz Kidz support team - our own little sub-team of my husband and me and our four dogs who enjoyed the training!

The Charity - Whizz-Kidz

Whizz-Kidz provides customised wheelchairs, tricycles and other specialised mobility equipment, wheelchair training, information and advice to change the lives of disabled children by giving them freedom and independence.

It is a charity whose work is very close to my heart. By supporting them I wanted to repay a debt to help disabled children and their parents: when my disabled son was alive many people helped me. Also, I experienced first hand the lack of individually designed mobility equipment and had to invent design and build it myself.

Between my husband and I, we raised over £12,500 for Whizz-Kidz and also raised lots of awareness for their work through our website.

Fundraising Tip

Put together an enthusiastic web-site diary (ours is www.rkb-law.com/kili) of all the training, the learning curves you experience, the ups and downs and then the trek itself. We sent it out (shamelessly and relentlessly!) to a huge mailing list requesting donations and keeping those who had already given updated. Also, consider contacting private charitable trusts early on so that they can fit a donation in to their yearly budget.

Diary

"The whole experience was total enlightened self-interest: the best thing I have ever done with my life benefitting a fabulous charity and fulfilling a dream and a promise to my lovely dead son."

Best Moments

From receiving the first £1000 cheque to completing a training circuit in 3 hours that had originally taken 7 hours, to the extraordinary night sky of the summit attempt with the stars and moon and moon shadows, to that Coca-cola back at base camp after the climb...nothing but highlights throughout the experience!

Hardest Moment

Forcing myself to the gym after work on a winter's day, dragging myself up Scafell Pike miles behind the rest of the team on a training weekend and the last four hours of the summit attempt when each step was an effort of will ... quite a few, really!

Biggest Problems

Training Tip - Invest in regular input from a personal trainer for professional advice and encouragement and don't underestimate how much harder the challenge itself will be.

I had very painful knees on the way down the summit itself but also down the training peaks of Ben Nevis and Snowdon, as well as arthritic pains in my right leg throughout training and trek, diarrhoea and vomiting for two days on the trek. We also regret only taking one "flavour" of antibacterial wipes for all purposes so that the smell became associated with all functions...!

Marina and her husband during their Kilimanjaro challenge

Fundraising ❷ Events

Fundraising events give you limitless potential to raise money. Sponsorship from family, friends and contacts may be fairly predictable but it is also finite. This is because such donations are not part of people's everyday expenditure so they cannot, or do not feel that they can, keep shelling out for charity. Socialising and having fun are part of this expenditure and people spend more freely on this than any other part of their lives. If you feel uncomfortable asking those you

The key to a successful fundraising event is the balance between raising money and giving people a good time. Even at charity events guests expect some value for money and still compare what they have received in terms of entertainment against what they have paid. If people feel good about this comparison, then they will be more willing to contribute more money to the cause on that occasion and at future events.

know to fork out extra cash then worry not, because they are already spending this money in bucket loads. Moreover, you have two advantages over other social events:

- You can give people a good time AND make them feel good about the money they have spent
- You can make a far larger profit from fundraising events by off-setting the costs through gift-in-kind sponsorship.

In terms of achieving the aims of your challenge in a broader sense and making an enduring contribution to your cause, events also offer two more advantages:

- Events are the ideal platform for raising awareness of the work of your charity
- By informing and enthusing your guests about your cause you are able to foster relationships with the charity, to which they are more likely to give again.

The Method

If the idea of organising and staging an event brings you out in a cold sweat then relax, because as with sponsorship, there is a process that you can follow to give you the best possible chance of success. To the following method add time, enthusiasm and persistence and you will find yourself on the end of a massive fundraising total.

10 Steps to a Successful Event

Getting money and support from people can be tough and there is no room for dithering and fretting. With time, thought and the right process you will surpass your target with ease. Approach this challenge as you would any problem and methodically break down the job in hand:

1. HELP, EXPERIENCE & EXPERTISE
2. BRAINSTORM & RESEARCH
3. DATE, VENUE & AUDIENCE
4. THEMES
5. MARKETNG & PUBLICITY
6. FUNDRAISING AT THE EVENT
7. ENTERTAINMENT
8. AWARENESS
9. EVENT PLAN
10. ORGANISATION

Ideas for Events

- Art exhibition – Get all the local/school/office artists to contribute paintings, drawings, photos and sculptures; frame them, mount them and make them look great, charge an entry fee then sell them.
- Battle of the Bands – There are aspiring bands and musicians everywhere. Get them all in one place, sell tickets and find a panel of top judges. If you can get a record label rep to come along you will up the profile and attract better bands.
- Beer Festival – Beers from around the county, the country or the world. Remember licenses.
- Board Games Evening – Collect together a range of classic and simple games, set time limits for each round and shower winners with sponsored prizes.
- Bingo – Simple and appealing
- Burns Night – Make an occasion of this annual Scottish tradition and take a cut of the ticket price.
- Carol Concert/Singing – Keep the quality of singing high and let that attract people, rather than endlessly rattling tins and following people around.
- Casino Night – A potentially great way to raise money. Make sure that there is something for everyone and that you have all the necessary permissions.
- Classic Car Show – Classic car enthusiasts normally overlap with the social bracket that give most money to charity. You will be surprised by how much interest there is.
- Coffee morning – Tried and tested means of community fundraising. Mums, grannies, aunties, friends – everyone knows how to hold a coffee morning.
- Concert – Find a way of contacting a well known or reputable band, orchestra or group of musicians and make them the centrepiece of a fundraising event.
- Cocktail Night – Tasty and usually expensive drinks made well and cheaply – a regular winner. Don't scrimp on your mixers and consider getting in some pro-barmen.
- Crossword Contest - This works with crosswords and riddles. Put together a tough sheet of puzzles, find a few sponsored prizes and send them out to people.
- Darts/Pool/Table Football Tournament – Indoor events which keep the costs down and demand zero preparation beyond turning up on the participants behalf.
- Eating Contest – Another popular theme. Find sponsors among restaurants and suppliers and hold a number of different contests: chillies, donuts, water biscuits. Ensure very high hygiene standards.
- Face Painting – Seems like it's just for the kids, but stand outside any big sporting event and you have thousands of punters looking to show their colours.
- Fancy Dress – Anyhow and anywhere, the fancy dress theme always makes

people relaxed and off-guard.

- Fashion Show – Potentially a massive winner. The key is developing lots of contacts amongst local fashion shops, designers and suppliers. Give the audience a chance to buy or order what they have seen and take a cut.
- Fete – Something for everyone at a village fete and an opportunity to pull together lots of small-scale fundraising ideas into one event
- Film Evening – Find an angle that differentiates the evening from an average night in watching tv: classic black-and-whites, films with local relevance, 80s classics etc.
- Firework Display – Always popular, but remember that people's standards are high and public shows are cheap and very impressive.
- Flower Show – Everyone loves flowers in summer. Get a whole band of suppliers together in a beautiful setting, charge a small entry fee and take a cut of the profits.
- Football/Tennis/Touch rugby Tournament – Target specific groups to put a team together: companies, teachers, clubs, associations etc.
- Go-Karting GP – Like paintballing, expensive to hold, but with the right participants and thorough research and organisation it can raise good money.
- Guess the Weight/Size/Amount – This one fits into any event as a nice sideline
- Karaoke Night – Gets more and more popular every year and cheap to put

on. Make sure it is well organised and structured – people hate a karaoke shambles.
- Lads/Ladettes Olympics – Made up of anything mainly unenergetic: drinking, eating, pool, penalty shoot out, table football etc.; put together a points system, find some prizes and charge for

The Non-Event This sounds like a cop out but it is a potential winner. Everything is in the invite: strike an amusing chord with people who feel obliged to attend a number of charity events every month. Let them know that on a certain date there is absolutely nothing going on, no dress code and no live music. Tickets to this totally unsociable evening are sold, with all the proceeds (i.e.100%) going to charity.

individual or team entries
- Mini-Olympics – Same theme as above, but based more on real sporting events, or parts thereof.
- Mufti Day – Ideal for a school; £1-2 to abandon uniform for the day and wear casual clothes
- Open Garden – Find a beautiful garden and ask if you can hold an open day for people to come and enjoy the environment. Set up a refreshments stall and hope for good weather.
- Paintballing – As this is quite an expensive activity you will have to generate some goodwill from suppliers to get a decent cut of the profits.
- Pancake Party – Any food theme will do: donuts, bagels, cookies etc. Ask

for help and contributions.

- Pantomime – Again, this works best as part of an institution or organisation: office, school, university, clubs etc. Good record for success
- Playstation Tournament – Lots of scope here to raise money and awareness within groups of young people.
- Pub Quiz – Well tried and tested and very successful if held regularly at a busy pub
- Talent Show – Same theme as the Battle of the Bands event, but with more variety. Include some up for it jokers, but make sure there are plenty of ringers too.
- Underwear Party – Less risqué than it sounds and it can actually generate a very chilled-out and fun atmosphere. Target the right groups.
- Wine Tasting – This can be pitched at any level and crowd. Develop relationships with suppliers and find ways of connecting what you are doing for them or their product: local consumers, country of origin etc.

"When you are coming up with ideas for events think about what groups of people you are planning to invite or market the event to. Put yourself in their shoes. What do they do with their time off? What kind of events do they often attend? Are there any shared interests amongst them? This will help you put on popular and successful events."

Head of Events, ICROSS

- Quiz Show – Very good fun and popular when they are organised well. Make the effort and find a well known theme.

Office Events

- Bad Hair/Dress Day – Themed days at the office can be a great way to get people involved. Suit the theme to

Work Themed Challenge – link charity donations to certain mistakes or achievements at work, such as spotting a health and safety hazard, being late for a meeting or reaching a sales target. This can be a big favourite with management, who should be willing to match donations.

your colleagues and think about what they would respond to.
- Beard & Moustache Shave – This can be a big money spinner as well-established office facial hair fetches a high price for public removal, especially among the managers.
- Crime Box – When anyone commits a minor office crime, like being late, swearing, or letting their phone go off in a meeting, then they get charged a small fee.
- Waxing – This one is for the boys. There will be a lot of interest and support from smug female colleagues.
- Dream Job Day – Colleagues pay to dress up as someone from their dream job.
- Green Day – Get as many people as possible to make the daily commute

by bike, on foot or as part of a car share, and the money they save on transport goes to your charity.

- Who's Who? – Collect baby pictures of everyone in the office and run a competition to guess who's who.

Make sure that whatever you are doing people know that all the profits are going to charity or if anything will be used towards expenses. Take advantage of the attention to raise awareness of your cause and tell people about what you are doing.*

Charity Sales Events

- Arts & Crafts Stall – Get good quality contributions from local producers and talented hobbyists. Attractive, simple jewellery can often be made very cheaply.
- 2nd Hand Clothes Sale – There are a vast number of people who have bags of clothes that they *"have been meaning to take to the local charity shop for ages."* Go round collecting and arrange the clothes into sizes when you present them.
- Book Sale – Same as above
- Cake Stall – Can be done anywhere. Piggyback a bigger event or gathering of people.
- Calendar – Scantily clad local icons always sell well. Do your market research and keep costs as low as possible.
- Car Boot Sale – Charge entry or take

a cut of the profits.
- Car Wash – If you can involve some attractive young men and women this fundraiser can pull in the crowds.
- Furniture Sale – Same as Second Hand Clothes sale.
- Odd Jobs – Gardening, cleaning, ironing, tutoring, babysitting, shoe shine etc.
- Recipe Book – Collect favourite recipes from relatives, neighbours, friends, restaurants and anyone that cooks well.
- Refreshments – Any event, gathering – get permission and make sure people know where the money is going.
- Recycling – Collect paper, scrap metal etc. and sell it to a recycling company.
- Unwanted Presents Sale – Great just after Christmas.

Check out all the legalities that will affect your event on page 93. If you have more specific queries or concerns, always ask your charity before ploughing ahead.

1. Find help, experience and expertise

Event organisation is an art in itself and demands experience to be really successful. Important lessons are learnt after organising any kind of event, from small dinner parties to an afternoon of corporate hospitality to major fundraisers. Consequently, there will undoubtedly be a number of people within your sphere of contacts that have excellent advice to offer.

Committee

The best way of mobilising this support is to form a committee. For a small, local fundraising event, this could be made up of the members of the team, a couple of parents, your brother and a few close friends.

Volunteers

A team of volunteers is essential for events and all charities have to develop a network of people who they can rely upon. People close to you will normally be happy to give their time and play a part in the success of the occasion. Try and accumulate a large number of volunteers, so that jobs can be divided up fairly and no-one is over burdened.

Event Organiser

For larger events, you may be able to secure the help of a professional event organiser for free and accumulate a number of other individuals who have contacts in each of the event's areas (food, music etc). If not for free, then consider taking one on at a reduced rate. Professional event organisers are a good investment if you have the resources, as they will know how to maximise the profits.

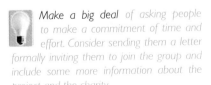

Make a big deal of asking people to make a commitment of time and effort. Consider sending them a letter formally inviting them to join the group and include some more information about the project and the charity.

"Volunteers are crucial to the success of a fundraising event: a good volunteer team will ensure your event runs smoothly and professionally. It's vital your volunteers feel a part of the event so get them involved early and include them in your plans, which also means you are more likely to benefit from their skills and contacts. On the day, make sure they are well briefed and don't forget to thank them afterwards to ensure they feel valued and appreciated."

Elizabeth Livesey-Haworth, Head of Events, Kids

2. Brainstorm and Research

Having formed a committe, however small, sit down and think about what you imagine the event or events to be. Ask yourselves how much money you want to raise, how much money you can invest upfront and how much time you have to organise it. Try and do a quick count of guaranteed and possible numbers. For example, if there are four of you and each can guarantee 50 guests and offer 50 more hopefuls, then look for a venue with a capacity of 250-350.

Secondly, you need to research some of the possibilities. Examine your list of contacts and link as many people as possible to the needs of an event. Then research previous fundraising events. Your charity will be able to offer advice and the events team there will have experience of events of all sizes. There are a number of other groups at your disposal that will be able to help, such as your local school, church, sports clubs and pubs. All of these groups regularly fundraise for themselves or local causes with small-scale events. If possible, attend a couple of fundraising events and keep an eye out for what you think has been done well and what could have been done better. Perhaps even speak to the organisers and ask if you can meet up for a drink, so that you can pick their brains and maybe get some useful contacts thrown your way.

When you are coming up with ideas try and think as broadly as possible. A fundraising event is not just a charity party or dinner. The best fundraising events are the imaginative and innovative. So think about what suits your resources and your target audience and be willing to introduce totally new ideas. Everything works with the investment of time and energy.

Type of Event

The type of event/s is clearly an important decision and there are a vast number of possibilities. The key is to offer people an imaginative and exciting idea and that is going to be profitable. Look through the special pages on ideas for events and consider this example of a successful portfolio of events.

An ambitious team of challenge fundraisers may be able to put together the following portfolio of events over the course of a year:

Party of 200 guests at a bar owned by a helpful contact. All charged £8 entry, which includes a free drink. A friend's band plays free of charge. £1000 after costs

University Fashion Show organised with local fashion stores and national chains in the area. All clothes donated and sold at end of event. £15 per ticket with 300 in the audience. £4000 raised after costs

Pub Quiz every Tuesday night at the local pub for three months before challenge. 15 teams at £10 each. £50 first prize, sponsored bottle of champagne second prize. 10% of bar takings during quiz. £2000 raised after expenses.

➤➤ Bad Hair Day at office. Employees pay £5 to wear ridiculous-looking hair styles to work. £300 raised.

➤➤ Mufti Day at local school. Pupils pay £1 to wear casual clothes instead of uniform. £250 raised

➤➤ Local Church holds a coffee morning for you after the Sunday service. £250 raised.

➤➤ Women's Institute's Wine Tasting. The local branch of the W.I. holds a wine tasting for its members, with the wine donated by the local merchant. 25 people at £15 per head. £300 raised after costs.

➤➤ A Congratulations Party held by the participants' family and friends on the completion of the challenge. £20 a ticket for 200 guests, including sponsored food, 2 drinks and 2 raffle tickets. Auction of promises and raffle. £4,500 raised after costs.

TOTAL EVENTS RAISE: £12, 500

3. Venue, Date & Audience

These essential details need to be decided upon as early as possible. When you have this, you can start to lay down firm plans, making bookings and inviting guests. Some of the aspects that you need to consider:

- Event - Fun/sophisticated/formal/informal, music, food, entertainment, fundraising methods, charity awareness

- Venue - Capacity, cost, facilities, location convenient for greatest number of people, parking, disabled access, safety, neighbours

- Date - Potential clashers, school holidays, relevance to the trip, weather, time available to organise, equipment availability

- Audience - Varied or grouped, number, age range, disposable income, tastes, social calendar

Maria Standen and her husband made over £3,500 towards their total of £11,500 for Cancer Research UK by putting on big fundraising events

4. Themes

People love themed parties. Why do you think that so many of the most successful club and bar chains are themed? Your project presents a range of opportunities to theme events imaginatively and relevantly. A theme also gives your event individuality, particularly if you come up with novel ideas. This adds considerably to your guests' sense of value for money, which makes them more willing to be generous on the night. Every one of them will be able to work out what they would get for the same price somewhere else in terms of food, drinks and music. If you give people an original and exciting experience, they cannot pigeon-hole this value as easily.

Themed events also provide an imaginative base for reducing your costs through the branding of different elements. A night of nibbles, beer and karaoke does not offer much scope for approaching companies with an original idea. Exciting ethnic food, music, decoration and even dress would be much more attractive.

Challenge Theme

This is a great way of getting your guests involved and interested in your project. Whether your challenge took you across seven South American countries or through four English cities, you can theme the food, the decorations and the music around where you are going or where you have been. Similarly, your activity could be the inspiration. Some disciplines, such as kayaking and swimming, lend themselves to particular themes, such as water. Others, such as road running, less so. However, think laterally: if you are taking on a triathlon then you could split the event into three clear areas or stages, or the meal into themed courses.

Cause Theme

Shaping the event around the overall purpose of the project is an imaginative way of raising awareness and demonstrating creativity. However, make sure you keep it tasteful and stick to simple themes. If you are raising money for Tommy's, the baby charity, then guests could sip cocktails through beakers and eat with their hands. If the cause is more political or sensitive and you have any doubts about whether it is appropriate then steer clear. If you have any doubts get advice from your charity.

Group Theme

If you are pitching an event at a particular audience or group then consider basing your event on their collective interest or identity, whether they are a rugby team, a common room of teachers or an office of IT specialists.

Keeping Costs Down

This is where your advantage lies and where you can really get stuck into that contacts list you developed at the start of the fundraising process. Everyone can offer some kind of gift-in-kind contribution to an event, so this is your chance to get all your friends, family, colleagues, local businesses and community groups involved. Think very broadly about everything you need and who could help you out with it, or start from the other angle and consider first what free resources you have access to and shape your event around these.

There are people out there who provide everything you need to stage an event – it is your job to use the means laid out in Fundraising I to solicit this support.

► Supermarkets often offer vouchers for local customers putting on a charitable event.

► A local farmer could provide a field for a car boot sale or a barn for a dance

► Local shops can be approached to offer services and prizes for your auction, raffle or competition

► Your local school, town hall or community centre could offer their communal rooms for a venue

► Musicians, dancers and DJs can provide free entertainment for an evening

► A local restaurant could be the venue for an event or the supplier of cost-price nibbles

For companies to provide a couple of hundred samples of their product and some promotional material for a charity event is very common. A friendly phone call to someone in the marketing and promotions department of a large company very often results in a generous response. If you can find a relevant reason to approach them (however contrived) and an angle for them to use this can be a great way of getting food, drink and event trimmings sponsored and raising the profile of the event.

► During your breaks from walking across England you scoffed Mars Bars to keep you going. A few photographs and a letter to follow up a phone call to the Mars marketing department results in 300 Mars Bars that can be used in a dessert at your welcome home party and a Mars banner that can serve as a colourful tablecloth.

► Whilst training for a trans-African cycle you have been constantly plugged into your i-Pod. In return for a few photographs of you using their equipment in the mountains, deserts and jungles of Africa, Apple agree to provide a new iPod for the raffle at your farewell fundraiser.

International Challenges

Remember to direct your appeal towards any businesses that reflect your international definition and can benefit from associating with your event.

- Importers - Products imported from countries on your route can be promoted at an event.
- Restaurants - Ethnic restaurants can use your event to promote their national foods. They will enjoy the opportunity to show off their culture and attract new customers.
- Bars and Clubs – Britain is covered with internationally themed bars and clubs. The more contrived venues are often keen to demonstrate their claim to ethnic authenticity. Those run by the ethnic minorities themselves will often be enthusiastic about your project and happy to help with supplies or a venue at a reduced rate.
- Tourist Boards and Embassies - Both of these are always looking for ways of encouraging travel to their countries. Your party presents an opportunity to provide decorations and also help with contacts for ethnic food and music.

5. Fundraising at the Event

Whether or not guests pay to attend the event or you are providing entertainment, you should still encourage them to contribute during the course of the day, afternoon or evening. The best way of doing this is to turn giving into a game, with tangible rewards for being generous, doing well or being lucky.

Tombolas

This is the simplest way of raising some money at low-key events and also for using small prizes and getting everyone involved. Essentially, a tombola consists of a table covered in prizes, labelled with numbers. The participant pays a small amount and then picks a ticket out of a "tombola" or bucket. At this point there are a few variations.

- The number on the ticket corresponds to a prize on the table, with all the winning numbers between, for example 50 and 100, so a full search is not necessary every time.
- Numbers ending in 0 or 5, for example, have been picked as the winning figures, so if you find one of these tickets you can choose a prize.
- Different groups of numbers represent different tiers of prizes. Numbers ending in 0 for top prizes, 5 for the second tier and 8 for the third, for example. This avoids the "tombola graveyard", when all that is left on the table is a tin of Brussel sprouts and a handkerchief.

Raffles

This is a great way to boost the income of events of any size. Accumulating prizes might appear to be the hardest element, but you will be surprised what people will offer you. Scan the list of Raffle/Auction prizes below for ideas.

A raffle may be done as part of an event or as a separate undertaking and this dictates how and when the tickets are going to be sold. If you are selling tickets over a period of time through a number of agents, then you must be organised. Names and contact details must be attached to each purchase, and every ticket needs to be clearly numbered and distinguishable. If it is a large-scale raffle then you need to ensure that the tickets are not reproducible. At an event, you need to be careful not to make mistakes with the tickets – selling both halves of numbered coupons is more common than you might think! As a safety measure, write down names on the back of your copy of the coupon. Demonstrate the prizes on offer as clearly as possible. Check the legal requirements surrounding raffles on page 93.

Highs and Lows

Every event is made up of a series of crests and troughs. You cannot expect to maintain the same level of excitement throughout. The point at which the participants are most stimulated, and therefore most generous, is at the top of these crests. When you are designing your event, imagine how the general mood varies with your programme of entertainment. Build a 'peak' moment well before the momentum of the whole occasion begins to wane. This is the point at which you make your major "ask" for support.

Auctions

Another tried, tested and very successful way of raising money. With the right group of people, and an exciting and relaxed atmosphere, you can benefit from a collective rush of impulsive generosity. All of a sudden pot plants will be going for £50 and you will be looking for more things to auction…curtain rails, tablecloths, anything!

Open auction

An auctioneer offers each lot and the participants bid by raising their hands or acknowledging the auctioneer in some way. This acts as a form of entertainment and a focus for everyone at the event, not just those bidding. It is also the format that suits charity events, where the lots are a chance for people to show off their generosity.

Tips

- A lot rests on the quality and personality of the auctioneer. Experienced and flamboyant auctioneers are able to create an atmosphere in which guests enjoy giving and thrive on the attention.
- The auctioneer needs an assistant to display the prizes and generate excitement.
- You need to have at least one "spotter" for every 10 to 20 guests. These helpers watch the bidders carefully. The closest "spotter" to the winner goes immediately to the person and get their details.
- If you are planning an auction at an event without a sit-down meal, then you need to make sure that one of the rooms is big enough for all the guests to gather. This may require a small stage and a PA system.

- The lots should be on display during the event, preferably with someone on hand to answer questions.
- There should be a clear list of the lots and the order in which they will be auctioned. Ideally, everyone in the audience should have a leaflet giving this information.
- Ask people to bring their cheque books as part of the invitation.

Blind Auction

This is the preferred option for auctions that are not live i.e. not during an event. However, they do work at events as well and can be quite exciting. The principle is that people place blind bids for auction lots, hoping that theirs is the highest. In its simplest form, the highest bid takes the prize.

Winner Pays Runner-up's Bid

This is often used for corporate acquisitions auctions and often brings the most profitable results. Basically, people are encouraged to bid beyond their means in the hope that they will win the bid, yet knowing that they will not have to pay that amount. The hope is that the second uppermost bid is still higher than the winner would have achieved in a conventional auction.

Dutch Auction

This is more suitable for auctions at smaller events, with less glitzy prizes. The auction of each prize is given an undisclosed amount of time, say between 10 and 30 seconds. During this time the auctioneer asks for small bids to be raised on the floor. If the first bid is £1 then that goes straight into a collection tin. If the second is £1.50, then the difference is contributed, so 50p in this case. The third bid could be £5, so the bidder would add £3.50. When the timer stops the last person to put money in the tin wins the prize.

Tips

- Make sure everyone understands the rules before you start
- You need one helper with a collection tin per ten people to keep things moving fast. Or, put a tin on every table and rely on people's honesty.
- Ask people to bring along change in the invite or give guests a chance to get change before you start.

Bingo

Everyone knows the concept and this is easy to organise. For added effect borrow a ball roller and use a PA system to announce the numbers. Charity bingo events are exempt from licensing, as long as the stakes and fee are no more than £3 and the total value of prizes does not exceed £300.

Ideas for Raffle/Auction Prizes

- Collectors items, one-offs or signed goods
- Promises of services: from DIY to financial advice to a beauty makeover
- Old stock in local shops
- Meals in pubs, restaurants and cafes
- Short breaks in hotels and B&Bs
- Flights and holidays
- Small-scale sponsorship from large companies
- Dinner with a celebrity
- 'Slave' auction
- Items related to the challenge – bikes, framed pictures etc

6. Marketing and Publicity

A decision that needs to be taken early on and will dictate how you market and publicise your event is whether or not you aim to open it up to the general public or just keep it within a private sphere of relatives, friends and contacts.

Private

- Send invitations of all kinds – e-mails, letters, postcards, text-messages. Be imaginative: the invitation is all the potential guest has to decide whether or not it will be worth going to.
- Set a ticket sales target for each member of your event committee
- Target groups of people at the same time, like the office or football team, so the event becomes a talking point. Never underestimate the sheep factor.
- Remind people as often as possible with posters, flyers and e-mails.
- Ask friends who have access to groups of potential guests to hand out flyers.

Public

- You need to commit resources to poster and flyer campaigns directed at specific audiences.
- For local events, target public community areas, like schools, post-offices, shops, libraries and high streets. Do not underestimate people's spontaneity: those with a free evening or afternoon might make a decision to attend on the day or even during the event. If you have the means to absorb these spur of the moment guests then consider putting a volunteer in charge of flyering during the event and publicise it in the area surrounding the venue.
- Get on event listings in the local/national press.
- Invite a radio station, magazine or newspaper, as they may consider covering the event and promoting it on air.

"Both public and private events need a hook. Your aim is to make people want to come, not just feel obliged to turn up and pay their money. This needs to be adapted to your target audience and could consist of anything that they cannot get on an average night out. Some examples: celebrity guests, live music, special entertainment, competitions, fireworks displays, circus performers, interactive displays. Make these enticements clear on the invite and make them sound exciting."

Head of Events, ICROSS

7. Entertainment

A good event is made up of a series of focuses. This can be done through food, drinks, dancing, decorations and awareness activities. How you can entertain your guests is also an important consideration. Here are some of the possibilities:

- Live Music
  - Bands
  - DJs
- Performers
  - Dancers,
  - Comedians,
  - Magicians,
  - Hypnosis

- Interactive entertainment
  - Drumming,
  - Dance lesson,
  - Group games
- Stalls
  - Games,
  - Challenges,
  - Trade tables

8. Awareness at Events

Your project is powerful as a vehicle for inspiring people to give and also to be informed. At an event you have the full attention of the guests for a certain period of time, so take advantage of it. A successful challenge project will not simply enable one-off donations for a particular charity, but instead inspire and foster a longer-term financial commitment and emotional engagement with the cause.

Again there are balances to strike here: give people the opportunity to find out without shoving it down their throats; demonstrate the importance of the issue without ruining the mood of the event. However passionately you believe that everyone should take notice of your cause, you do not want to make people feel guilty about having a good time, or resentful about being patronised. Here are some ideas:

Displays

Imaginative and colourful displays showing the work of the chosen charity make people aware of the importance of their presence at the event. Make them accessible, interesting, easy to read and based upon human experiences – remember that sympathy is central to charitable giving. Interlink pictures and text with details of your project: beforehand this could be route maps and the implications of your fundraising target; afterwards you should have accumulated a variety of materials,

s and diaries. The
...ploy the better, so
...a loop for example
...nt reminder and piece

Presenta... ...s

Again, the key is to do things in an

"Events are a great occasion to raise awareness and we always try to get people's attention and let them have some information about our work. Engaging people about our charity and talking to them about the problems and solutions helps us recruit new supporters and having a campaign action to sign up to works well for us."

Raj Dasani, Fundraiser, Anti-Slavery International

imaginative and entertaining way. Guests will understand why they are there and will be happy to find out more by listening to a speech or watching a short video, but they will not respond well to being lectured. See page 135 for advice on giving presentations.

Flyers, Leaflets and Publicity Material

If you can get guests to take something home to remind them of their evening in a constructive way (not food poisoning, for example!) then you have another means of fostering that more substantial link to the cause. Consider handing promotional material out as they leave.

9. An Event Plan

Creating a plan of the event is vital. "Turn up, mingle, drink, nibble, dance and leave" is not sufficient. A successful event will guide the guests through a schedule, which may be very subtle and simple, but allows you to shape movement and mood to your advantage.

To start this plan draw a list of objectives for the event and sketch the layout of the venue. These then need to be matched to create a timeline. This end result clearly varies according to the nature of the event. A fashion show, for example, demands a totally different plan from a village fete. However, there are a number of factors that apply to all:

- Create a welcoming and relaxed environment to ease guests in as they arrive. Take their coats, give them a drink and direct them to an area in which to mingle early on, for example.
- Give the event a series of focuses and, if possible, one main episode

that acts as a centrepiece for fundraising and awareness.
- Develop the event with surprises which maintain the attention of the guests. This could be done through the venue, by gradually revealing various stages and areas, using simple tricks with curtains and lighting and incorporating all your assets – music, food, speeches, videos, special guests.
- Think about where you want the guests to be at certain points of the event and how you will get them there. Consider food, drink, speeches, presentations, raffles, auctions and other entertainment and focuses.

10. Organisation

There is no problem with being ambitious with your events. However, your ambition and enthusiasm has to be matched by your organisation. Here are all the aspects that you need to consider:

Insurance

This needs checking thoroughly, as being caught out will have major implications for your project. All venues need Public Liability insurance and you may need additional cover depending on what type of event you are holding. If you are bringing in suppliers these too need insurance. Most insurance companies will run through exactly what you need and give you a quote.

Health and Safety

The regulations surrounding public events become more extensive every year, just as lawsuits for negligence become more common. If you are hiring premises the manager or owner must run through all the health and safety issues. If you use your own premises, you need to cover all aspects thoroughly: do a risk assessment and abide by all regulations.

Security

You need to ensure the security of your guests, their possessions, all money taken on the day, the venue itself and all equipment and materials. If you need to hire security then they need to be registered with the local council, who will have information about requirements and sources.

Facilities

It is of course essential that you provide guests with enough toilet facilities. No-one wants to spend half the event queuing. Other essential facilities are safe and manned cloakrooms, free drinking water and easy access to fresh air.

Accessibility

There are two important reasons why you need to make your events totally accessible to people of all disabilities. The first is that it is now a legal obligation to make public events fully accessible. The second is that a good challenge project should have a positive impact in every sense. Your events should therefore be model examples of accessibility and inclusion. Remember, access is not simply a question of physical passage for wheelchair users. Only 8% of registered disabled people in the UK use wheelchairs and the rest have a wide variety of needs. These needs can best be met with common sense and simplicity: large writing, clear signage, transparent language.

Tickets

These can either be sold on the door or before the event. If you have resources for marketing and advertising beforehand then this is preferable, as you have money up front to use for expenses, you have a better idea of the numbers and you save time and energy on the day. Once you receive the money, add the individual to your fundraising spreadsheet and keep a separate list for the door. Give yourself a cut-off point for sending out tickets by post and also consider using e-mail confirmation. If tickets are sold on the night then you need a system for their purchase, with enough volunteers dedicated to the job. If you have a combination of pre-sales and day sales then separate the sale itself and the checking of tickets/guest list, just as all large venues do.

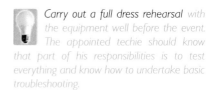

Consider offering benefits to those buying tickets before the event, such as a discounted price or a free drink or raffle ticket. You will ultimately save money and create a better event if you know how many people are coming, particularly in terms of food and drink.

Arrival

You need a clear process for this, which must include definite means for: finding the venue and entrance, parking cars if applicable, welcoming the guests, the checking/purchase of tickets, taking of coats and bags and pointing people in the right direction. Only very huge events need more than one point of entry, so keep it focused unless absolutely necessary.

Equipment

It is unlikely that you will be able to put on any event without the use of electrical equipment. Even if this only consists of an extra fridge and a stereo, then it is still useful to appoint a volunteer to be responsible for its setting up, use, safety and packing up. The more comprehensive your equipment requirements, the more expertise you will need – if the PA system cuts off half-way through a speech or the video goes fuzzy at the vital moment then someone must be on hand to attend to the problems.

Carry out a full dress rehearsal with the equipment well before the event. The appointed techie should know that part of his responsibilities is to test everything and know how to undertake basic troubleshooting.

Contingency

Alternative plans are vital, as anything that relies upon so many people doing the right things at the right time is inherently unpredictable. Consequently, you must think through worst-case scenarios for every aspect of the event and come up with plans for their resolution. The main elements that require such attention are as follows:

Too many guests

The invitation process for events is often imprecise. Unless you have sold all the tickets beforehand, or are willing to enforce a guest list rigorously, then you will not know exactly how many people will arrive unannounced. You need to know exactly what your maximum capacity is and, if necessary, organise a one-in, one-out system.

Weather

All events that rely upon fine weather must have a realistic contingency plan, particularly in the UK. These vary from marquees at the expensive end, to a few gazebos for the low budget event.

Emergencies

As part of your health and safety obligations you will have to be accountable in major emergencies.

Being let down

It is dangerous to rely too heavily on individual people or resources. Good planning allows for certain aspects of the planning to fail without the impact being too consequential for the overall success of the event.

Volunteer Brief

Putting together a brief or crib sheet for everyone involved in the event can be time consuming for large undertakings, but it is essential. This needs to be divided up into three sections: information, tasks and schedule. Firstly, you must give all the information required by the volunteers, including a basic outline of the event, clear directions to the venue and travel options if applicable, as well as a summary of their general obligations as a group. Then you need to list the volunteers, their tasks and the times at which they will be required, followed by a description of these tasks. Finally, the schedule should mirror the plan that you have made for the event and translate it into timings, actions and people. Make sure that volunteers get an opportunity to enjoy themselves as well, and that you schedule break time if they have to perform a function that will be running throughout.

The Event Itself

Events are indeed all in the planning, so if this has been done well, then you should be able to rely upon it on the day, even if something goes horribly wrong. The most important thing is that the main protagonists of the challenge are available to their guests.

This means that you should appoint a co-ordinator. At this stage a professional events manager comes into their own, as they thrive on the immediate pressure on making things happen and co-ordinating a plethora of needs and goings-on.

Finances

A number of different people are spending money on a variety of things, there are petty cash sums being used in pressured moments, money is being collected from guests when the booze has been flowing and there are 14 other things to do. A system of event accounting is essential and it must be known and followed by everyone who comes into contact with money at any point, even for a short time.

Collecting Money

Collecting cash straight from the general public in tins and buckets is a very common way of raising money for charities. The methods vary from wacky antipodeans in tutus shouting at commuters to little old ladies from the church committee hovering in shopping centre lobbies.

Over the last few years this form of up front fundraising has become less popular as charities have latched onto the short-term benefits of face-to-face soliciting of direct debit agreements. However, for independent fundraising projects there is still a lot of potential in bucket collections. Here are some general principles for making them work:

- Plan a long way in advance and apply early to local authorities for Street Collection permits.
- Stay within the law: you are not allowed to talk directly to individuals or approach them; wear official ID badges; use sealed buckets; get the right permits; get permission for collecting on private property; make sure all collectors are over 16. (details on page 93)
- Choose areas which represent a balance between high foot fall (numbers of passers-by) and conspicuousness.
- Generate interest amongst the target group immediately before the collection. For example:
  - Stage an awareness event
  - Put up posters or advertise in the local media
  - If you get coverage of any sort e.g. regional television, then follow it up with local collections.
  - Get an announcement at a major event, such as a football match and then collect as people leave.
  - Create a scene (legally!)
  - Pick an occasion when there is some excitement and goodwill that you can take advantage of.
- Try to make people immediately aware of why you are there and what your project is about – confusion as to why you are raising money will be the first reason not to give.
- Make people want to give with your enthusiasm and charm.
- Try to avoid too much negative pressure i.e. making them feel uncomfortable about not giving. This generates bad feeling towards your charity and the voluntary sector as a whole.
- Ask local businesses if they will consider keeping a collection tin for you and putting up a poster.

Be **INFORMED** – there is nothing worse than asking questions of someone who knows little about the cause.

Be **CONFIDENT** – what you are doing is very worthwhile. If people scowl or mock then they are self-opinionated, pompous arses.

Be **GENUINE** – the British tend to be cynical about artificial wackiness

Be **POLITE** – this is very much appreciated by all potential donors.

As an inspirational example of charity challenge fundraising to motivate you through the difficult moments of fundraising, there is no-one better than the extraordinary Lloyd Scott.

Lloyd Scott joined the London Fire Brigade in 1985 and two years later received a commendation for rescuing two children from a house in Dagenham, Essex. After undergoing routine tests for toxic smoke inhalation it was discovered that Lloyd had Chronic Meyloid Leukemia.

Three weeks before his bone marrow transplant operation he ran his first marathon and just 11 months afterwards he ran again, after a long and hard recovery. Since then, Lloyd has completed the Snowdonia Marathon, the Everest Marathon and a 145 mile stage marathon through the Sahara Desert, as well as expeditions to both poles and a 135 mile ultra marathon through Death Valley, the hottest place on earth.

Although undergoing highly intensive chemo

Lloyd Scott crosses the finish line of the London Marathon after over five days of walking in a full deep seas diving suit

and radiotherapy treatment and being forced to have a hip replacement operation in 2000, Lloyd has continued to demonstrate unheard of resilience and bravery.

More recently he has added some imaginative twists to his challenges, completing the London and New York marathons in a deep sea diving suit, which he wore while traversing the bed of Loch Ness. In December 2004, Lloyd returned to England from Australia, where he had cycled from Perth to Sydney on a Penny Farthing bicycle. In 2005 he has completed another first - swimming from Land's End to John O'Groats in a pool being towed on the back of a truck. He has raised almost £4 million for the charity Children with Lukemia and in 2005 was awarded an MBE as part of the Queen's Birthday Honours List.

Taking Advantage of the Internet

The Internet holds endless potential for every aspect of charity challenge projects, from training to fundraising, so make sure you take advantage of it.

- **Ideas and Research** – There are reams of challenge events and expeditions out there, as well as thousands of independent sites, each one providing a new idea of what is possible.

- **Shared Experience and Expertise** – From hiking techniques to staging fundraising events to crossing African borders, someone has done what you are doing and shared their invaluable experience with the world

- **Fundraising** – Quick, reliable and tax efficient. Soliciting and collecting sponsorship online is a must for challenge fundraisers

- **A Focus** – A dedicated website or a page on a related site is essential for independent projects and highly recommended for any challenge: provide a reference point for interested parties; provide updates on every aspect of your progress; give recognition to key supporters; share what you have learnt.

Your Own Piece of the Web - Options

Basic - A Fundraising Page

Setting up a page to gather sponsorship is simple and this service is provided by large charities or sites such as *www.justgiving.com* and *www.bemycharity.com*. You can provide details of your challenge and what you hope to achieve and get a link that can be attached to sponsorship requests with ease. These pages give your supporters the option of leaving messages alongside their donation, helping create a small community around your challenge.

Intermediate - "Piggybacking"

By setting up a page within another website, you gain many of the benefits of a dedicated site without any of the hassle. This can be done on a number of different sites linked to you and your challenge: the charity, your place of work, any clubs, groups or associations you belong to, your old school and your sponsors.

Advanced - A Dedicated Website

This takes time, skill and money, but offers huge advantages. If you have access to the skills needed to design, set up and maintain a site with no support, then the sky is your limit. There are also websites that provide ready-made templates and step-by-step instructions for novices.

A Dedicated Site - What should it include?

You must decide early on exactly what you want your website to do and who you think will be accessing it. Consider the following questions:

1. Why will people be visiting the site and how will they have found out about it?

Divide these people into categories. For example: **a)** friends and family **b)** potential supporters/sponsors **c)** interested parties, such as guests at fundraising events, people who hear about the project or read your promotional material **d)** random web traffic

2. What do these people want to know?

- Friends and family – regularly updated personal information about you, the project and your progress
- Potential supporters/sponsors – how they can support you as an individual or company and what the potential benefits there are for them and the charity
- Interested parties – what are the aims and details of your project; how they can get involved

3. What else would you like visitors to know?

- As much as possible about your charity and its work
- All the ways in which they can support you – donations, events etc.
- That your project is serious, professional and creative

Content

Main sections:
- The Challenge/Aims – lays out clearly and succinctly what your challenge project involves, why you are doing it and what you aim to achieve
- The Charity – a summary of the work of your charity and how you hope to contribute to it. This should include a link to their site.
- Participants – a photo and brief biography of all the participants
- Sponsors – a list of individuals and organisations that want recognition, including a brief summary of the valuable role that each corporate sponsor is playing with a link to their site.
- Route – a map of where you are going
- Diary and Photographs – progress reports, diaries and up to date information and visuals from all aspects of the project – training, events, the challenge etc. People love photos, so include as many as possible.
- Events – a list of any event that people can attend (fundraising or awareness)
- "Support Us" – a donation page or link thereto and a downloadable sponsorship form.
- Contact details – yourselves and your charity

Possible extras:
- Message Board – friends, family and supporters will love the opportunity to post messages of support and they add considerably to the site.
- Video footage – posting short video (mpeg) files that visitors can download is less complicated than you might think

Make your site entertaining. Getting people to your site is one thing, but keeping them there and getting them to return relies upon the content. No matter what the scale of your challenge is, you can include creative, interesting and amusing material on your site. Consider including lots of photos, quotes, maps, diagrams and visuals.

Updating

Internet users want up-to-date information and if they find it on a site, they will come back again and again. Make a priority of updating the site with progress reports, diaries, photographs and messages as often as possible.

Consider including:
- A fundraising diagram, showing your target and progress
- A progress diagram on a map, so people can check how you are doing
- The day after each event, put photos up on the site and let guests know about them – this will increase regular traffic
- A short message update – a couple of sentences on recent events and your progress

On the occasions when you cannot update the site yourself don't let it fall by the wayside. Ask a friend or supporter to receive information from you and post it on the site. For short daily updates, consider text messages and phone calls, for longer ones, e-mails or packages of film or video footage.

How to get people to visit your website

- **Links** – Any link to or from your site will increase its web traffic. Think about every possible associated party that might be interested in having a reciprocal link. It is also an incentive to potential sponsors.

- **Exposure** – Get the site's name everywhere and include it on all your literature and promotional material. Make sure it is clearly visible and easy to read. Consider making cards with brief details of the project and a plug for the website. Talk about the site in any interviews you do and ask journalists and presenters to give it a mention.

- **Search Engine Marketing** – This involves advertising with the big search engines, but you can also use "meta-tags" to pull yourself up search engines' results lists, when your key terms and phrases are being searched.

Awareness

Awareness is king within the voluntary sector and your project is the ideal platform for spreading the word. Every year charities invest vast resources into increasing awareness of their cause and their organisation's brand. By taking on a challenge you are putting both the cause and the brand in the public eye. Your dedication and bravery illustrate their importance, your professionalism strengthens their credibility and your creativity and enthusiasm magnetise their image. Never miss an opportunity to raise awareness as it is potentially one of the most valuable legacies of your challenge.

The Importance of Awareness

The value of public awareness for charities is enormous. As this guide has emphasised, people are inspired to give by an emotional reaction to a cause. The more exposed they are to this cause, the more they understand about it and the more it becomes a part of their lives, the more likely they are to support it with money and energy as well as inspire others to recognise its importance.

Beyond the immediate incentives for charities of increasing awareness of their brand, there are also broader reasons why spreading information about the problems they address and their work in tackling these is so constructive.

Firstly, success stories from a voluntary sector that is striving for a better future make people feel more positive about progress in our society. The media is full of negative stories and messages, yet everyday amazing things are being done by charities around the world. Awareness of this work helps dispel the myth that these issues are doomed to be our society's sore thumbs forever.

Secondly, supporting charity is only a part of what people can do to affect social problems. We make hundreds of decisions every day, from how much water we use to what we buy at the supermarket to where and how we work to how we interact with people, and every one of them is a potential contribution to the same issues that charities address with their resources. By being aware of the social problems and issues that lie at the heart of the voluntary sector,

people have a better understanding of their own role in social change. This applies to the work of almost every charity and there are also organisations and campaigns that exist solely to raise this kind of popular awareness and through this effect change.

The Make Poverty History campaign does not aim to raise money but instead to raise awareness of the key issues affecting global poverty and, crucially, of the role that every indivudal has in changing them. By engaging millions of people around the world and prompting action, the campaign has not only inspired an understanding of issues such as trade justice and the debt burden, but also created a popular consensus around the need to address them.

A gathering of world leaders at the G8 Summit, 2005 (photo: Tony Adamson, Oxfam)

Your Potential to Raise Awareness

The contribution you will make to your charity through raising money is, without doubt, crucial. Every single pound counts. However, as an independent fundraiser your means are limited. No-one expects you to be able to raise infinite funds and transform your charity overnight; but when it comes to raising awareness and the impact that this has, your potential is limitless. If you raise £5,000 but also let 1000 people know why your cause is so important, then your contribution could ultimately spiral into hundreds of thousands of pounds and help instill far better general understanding of the central issue.

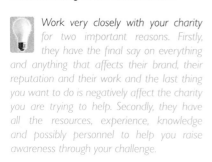 *Work very closely with your charity for two important reasons. Firstly, they have the final say on everything and anything that affects their brand, their reputation and their work and the last thing you want to do is negatively affect the charity you are trying to help. Secondly, they have all the resources, experience, knowledge and possibly personnel to help you raise awareness through your challenge.*

"Charity challenges are a great way of raising awareness. The London Marathon, for example, has 35,000 participants, a crowd of over 500,000 and a television audience of millions. This creates an ideal platform for drawing attention to our work which benefits greatly from wide public awareness of human rights abuses occurring around the world."

Amnesty International UK

Dedicated Awareness Challenges

A challenge project is such a good way of attracting attention to a cause that there is great potential in simply taking one with the sole aim of raising awareness. If you do not want to go through the fundraising process and are happy to cover all your own costs, then an awareness challenge is ideal.

How to make the most of dedicated awareness challenges:

- Consult your charity to find out exactly what will be the most beneficial and productive way of raising awareness for their work
- Be just as thorough in planning your campaign as you would be if you were aiming to hit a fundraising target
- Publicise the fact that you are covering all your costs yourself, that you are not asking for money and that you want people's attention in return for your efforts.

Ludkan Baba, or the Rolling Baba as the western media call him is a sadhu, or Hindu ascetic who has rolled (yes rolled) thousands of miles to bring peace to the world. Baba finished his sixth yatra in 2004, rolling 800 miles from his home in India's central Madhya Pradesh state to the Pakistani city of Lahore, to meet President Pervez Musharraf and urge him to reach a lasting peace with India. Surrounded by his disciples, the Rolling Baba rolls down the middle of the road, wearing only a blue t-shirt, some shorts, wrist bands and some stretch bandages on his upper legs and forearms.

Challenge Profile:

London Marathon for Amnesty International

Dr David Nicholl

Born 1965 – Consultant Neurologist

The Challenge: 'Running for Justice' 2005 London Marathon dressed as a Guantanamo detainee

The London Marathon is a very high profile event that was taking place three weeks before the General Election, which was an ideal time to raise awareness of the British residents still being held in Guantanamo as well as raise money for Amnesty International. I ran in an orange jump suit and a set of chains. The image I was trying to create was very much like the little girl in red in "Schindler's List" - in London I was one runner in Guantanamo kit out of 30,000 others. I spent ages searching the Internet for an appropriate outfit that I would be able to run in, then I managed to find a US medical supplies company that sold orange surgical scrubs- they are based in George Bush's home state of Texas!

My time was 4 hours and 43 minutes.

The Charity - Amnesty International

Amnesty International (AI) is a worldwide movement of people who campaign for internationally recognized human rights.

I have been an Amnesty member for years. Growing up in Belfast, I saw the effect of internment. I wanted to show that the first casualty of the 'War on Terror' was human rights.

Humour is a fantastic way to get people to think of even a very complex issue such as Guantanamo Bay. I did this in 2 ways: by singing Englebert Humperdink's "*Please Release Me*" en route (see photo) and by shouting out at the end of each mile "*Only another 25 miles of torture to go*". I also had a very loud whistle to draw attention to myself for those who were colour blind.

There is just so much competition for media space on the actual day of the marathon so the trick is to develop your media build-up BEFORE the marathon. For example, do a training run in your fancy dress into the middle of your local town etc and hope the press turn up. I have been covered in 20 different national and local media, including the Times newspaper and BBC News 24.

Diary

Best Moment
On the day of the Marathon was lucky enough to meet Terry Waite.

Hardest Moment
The day before the marathon when I, and the relatives of 3 Guantanamo families, were refused access to Number 10 Downing Street, and having to negiotate with the Police without getting myself arrested!

Training Tip
Start running! Follow a marathon training programme (Runners' Worlds are great), and build up with a 10km and half-marathon as part of your training. Get decent kit (especially shoes and socks- I have yet to ever get a blister!).

Biggest Problem
I suffered a knee injury 3 weeks before the marathon (iliotibial band syndrome) when I felt like Paula Radcliffe in the Athens Olympics, and it all looked like it was going pear-shaped. Luckily, my physio Emma, (physio with British Netball team) saved the day — it's the one time in my life I've pulled all the NHS connections I had to get the end result!

Fundraising Tip
Set up a Justgiving web-page. Change the page regularly and use it as a point of contact for everyone from friends to journalists. Give regular e-mail up-dates of progress.

"Running the marathon taught me how to turn my anger into activism. Apathy is the greatest global evil, don't get apathetic, get active!"

Dr David Nicholl sings "Please Release Me" during the London Marathon to the surprise of fellow participants

How to raise awareness

Just as effective fundraising can to be broken down into simple stages, so you can do the same thing when it comes to raising awareness. Once you understand this process you will be able to take advantage of every opportunity that presents itself.

Knowledge and Understanding

To achieve what you want to for your charity you will need to be prepared. Media interviews and large-scale presentations are two of the best means of raising awareness, but both demand a good knowledge of the short-term results of your contribution to the charity and the long-term implications of their work. This understanding is the first step in raising awareness, not least because it will probably make you more passionate about the organisation's work and this will be reflected in everything you do. Your charity is the first port of call for this, so look for some of the following resources:

- Annual reviews, newsletters and pamphlets
- Website information
- Press cuttings
- An example of a general application document (if permitted)
- Any literature or material surrounding the charity's key issues

 Explore ways of making your project topical. How does it fit in with prevailing political and social issues? Why should the challenge make more of a mark this year rather than last?

Key Messages

As an individual or small team with limited resources and, most probably, a limited period of people's attention to work with, it is best to determine at the outset what specific message you want to communicate. Delivering a single, powerful message consistently can be more valuable than attempting to cover everything. Within the voluntary sector the amount of time and money spent on campaigning varies enormously. However, central to the work of all charities is an issue or a number of issues. Each issue may have a number of sub-areas, any one of which you and your charity may feel suits your project best.

Resources

Your awareness work will predominantly go hand in hand with your fundraising efforts. There is also scope to go beyond this and undertake specific awareness projects, for example, by doing a lecture tour to present your experiences and the work of your charity. For both you need to collect a wide-range of resources that give details and deliver powerful messages about the key issues that you want to promote.

Once you have resources concerning the work of your charity, these need to be linked to those you have put together for your challenge. A well devised and planned challenge fundraiser links the challenge to the cause at every available opportunity. Make the most of this relationship and use it to bring the best out of each.

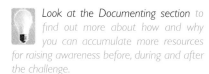 Chris Fields' Cycling Without Borders project, raising money and awareness for Medecins Sans Frontières, set up a website that offered three streams of information for every country that they cycled through: a diary of their progress, details of the MSF projects in that area and local and national political news and information.

Look at the Documenting section to find out more about how and why you can accumulate more resources for raising awareness before, during and after the challenge.

Fundraising and Awareness

The need to combine your plans for these two aspects of the project is clear. Firstly, by raising awareness, you increase the potential for interest and support. Secondly, fundraising brings you into contact with hundreds or thousands of people, every one of whom becomes an audience for information, even if it is only fleetingly.

Never miss an opportunity to raise awareness when you are fundraising and never miss an opportunity to fundraise when you are raising awareness.

Key Awareness Targets

There are three main areas upon which you can focus awareness work and it is useful to divide them up as they all demand a different approach.

- Everyone and Anyone – You end up talking to so many people about what you are doing in the build up to your challenge, so don't miss the chance to tell them why and how important it is to you.

- The Media – This provides the potential for the greatest exposure and there are opportunities all over the place for coverage if you look hard enough.

- An Audience – Presentations, lectures and events are the ideal way to hold people's attention, inspire and inform them.

The Media

The British media is always accused of being fickle and sensationalist, but if you approach them in the right way then the profile of the project could be raised tremendously through press, radio and television coverage at many different levels. Just ask yourself – what makes your project worthy of coverage through a particular medium? Your chosen charity may be able to offer some help with contacts and leads, but you may well have to predominantly develop your own angles and contacts.

Local Media

The main advantage of starting with local media is that it will be far more open to suggestions than at national level. They will respond to your ideas and will be more willing to give attention to the aspects that are important to you. Ideally, you want to organise your coverage to give maximum benefit to local fundraising work. If people read an article in the paper, hear something on the radio and watch a feature on local BBC news about your endeavour and then see you in person collecting money in the town centre or on a Saturday or making a brief appearance at the local football club, then they are more likely to make a donation and offer support. The elements that need to be assembled for local media attention in advance of your challenge date are:

A Press Release

Structure
Para 1
- Begin with a 20-30 word punch – this is the only part of the release that many people will read and will make up their mind about whether to read on and find out more.
- Make your project, its launch or its completion, an event upon which they can focus a topical news article.

Para 2
- Outline the piece of news in brief, pushing local relevance, whether it is cause, route or personally related.

Para 3
- Give a quote from yourself and if possible from someone with a high profile, like a local celebrity or important figure.

Para 4
- Give means of action – how people can get involved, find out more information or support you.

Editor's Notes/Additional Information
- Use this to provide journalists with any information that they might need for their article. Include
  - Relevant information about the individuals in the group
  - More details about the work of your charity
  - Dates for local appearances or events, with details of how you hope people might get involved or offer support (giving a donation, buying a ticket, listening to a presentation)

"If the information in your press release is imaginative, comprehensive and precise then journalists, researchers and editors will respond to it; mainly because they do not have to spend a lot of time investigating more information and coming up with angles. Give them the angles and the information on a plate."

Mark Hodgkinson - Journalist

Publicity photographs
Remember that a great picture may be enough to get you included, so attach some good quality sample photos to your press release. Include:

- A simple of shot of the team together
- A more creative picture of the training or preparation
- A picture with local relevance

Targets

Find out about the tone of the media you are hoping will cover you and consider adapting the press release and pushing a different angle of the trip. For example, there may be a programme on a local radio station that covers mainly women's issues, which makes your charity's work against breast cancer particularly relevant. Similarly, the sports editor of a local paper may give space to extreme physical challenges, in which case the adventurous part of your project will be more important to him.

Then get in touch with a journalist or researcher and get talking to them about what you are planning. Be enthusiastic and show how important attention from your local community is to you and how important what you are doing is to the community. You will have a press release and some photos on hand to send or e-mail and the person will know it is coming, which makes a massive difference. Ring back and follow up the letter or e-mail and offer any more information.

Try and offer exclusives to the sources that would be willing to make a real feature of your project, with promotion and follow ups.

 See some example press releases on the website.

National media

National exposure should be approached after as many local options as possible have been explored. Firstly, because you will gather confidence and momentum and secondly, because national papers and stations often pick up particularly interesting regional news. The angle at which the national media approaches your project will normally be completely different. The context and the audience no longer provide you with the chance of exposure simply because of where you are from, so the priorities laid out in your press release must be adapted, and the importance of some aspects of your project need to be slightly exaggerated.

Challenge projects can be picked up nationally for all sorts of reasons, one of

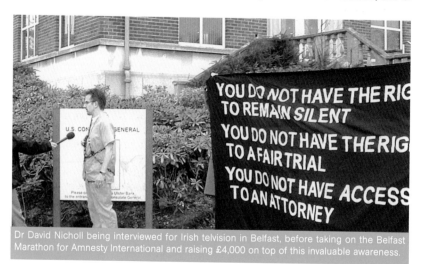

Dr David Nicholl being interviewed for Irish telvision in Belfast, before taking on the Belfast Marathon for Amnesty International and raising £4,000 on top of this invaluable awareness.

which may be that there could be very little news filling the papers and editors are looking for human-interest stories. Alternatively an element of your project may catch the imagination of a features editor or your cause could be particularly relevant.

All of these possibilities are worth investigating and along with the options described on page 130, they can form the basis of your plans for a press release and your targets. Blanket and ill-conceived press releases waste time and cause frustration in making little headway.

Ultimately, national media coverage could give your challenge a vast following, with thousands of hits on your website, hundreds of donations and scope for great sponsorship deals. However, be realistic. This very rarely happens, and when it does, it is normally in response to an absolutely extraordinary and original challenge or some kind of celebrity involvement.

It is unlikely that the media will share the same goals for your charity challenge project as you. Coverage can therefore become dominated by a sensationalist angle that may actually undermine what you are trying to achieve with the project. This means that you have to work hard to promote the information that is important to you and avoid attracting media attention for the wrong reasons.

The River Ganges Source to Sea expedition, led by Suresh Paul, set out to cover 1500 miles of the Ganges in 80 days by open canoe and white water raft. This inclusive (including disabled and non-disabled team members) expedition was organised and executed impeccably and at its heart were very commendable principles. They aimed to broaden awareness of inclusive outdoor activities and supported Water Aid to link the expedition and the chosen cause: the team felt they gained so much from being able to have access to water and travel on and enjoy it, that they should invest in access to water for those deprived of it. The team also undertook comprehensive volunteering and awareness work, attending the Ganges Water Rally, volunteering at the school for the deaf in Calcutta and donated expedition equipment and boats to NGOs in Calcutta.

However, during the expedition the team was violently attacked by bandits during the night. From this point all the media coverage of the project became dominated by this event, which distracted from its really valuable legacy as well as undermining the team's post-expedition fundraising efforts.

"The first expedition talk was to 1000 young people in Nottingham. However, the media published front-page news entirely on the attack. We decided after this to cancel the tour of talks as we did not want such a negative message to become the focus or be conveyed to young people in association with expeditions and Water Aid. This was a huge personal blow."

Suresh Paul, Designer and Outdoor Sports Coach

Interviews

If you get interviewed for local or national media then make the most of it.

- Be Prepared - Find out as much as you can about what areas the interview is going to cover in advance and research the possible answers. Find examples or quotes to add spice to your answers.

- Be Enthusiastic - If you don't come across as excited about what you are doing and passionate about its consequences then you have little chance of encouraging others to be.

- Take Advantage of the Attention - Make sure that readers, listeners or viewers know exactly what to do if they are interested in your project or your cause. Regularly mentioning a website address, for example, and asking the journalist or reporter to do the same can be very productive.

Presentations, Talks and Lectures

With your challenge you are demonstrating something remarkable. You should feel confident about telling people about what you are planning, what you are going through and what has been achieved. These presentations, talks and lectures can happen before, after and possibly during the challenge, and are a fantastic way of increasing awareness of your cause and interest in your project.

Awareness events of all kinds inspire others to offer help. In an audience of 50 people, there may be contacts and potential supporters. Awareness events often produce and fuel lots of leads for funds in other areas, as well as spreading the word about your cause.

Schools

Educationally, there could not be a better way of getting children involved in charities and good causes, as your adventure provides an imaginative and exciting medium for them. Community service and voluntary work can be presented as a drab obligation. For a fifteen year old boy, desperate to be outside kicking a football towards the girls' corner of the playground, Sunday visits to the old people's home and church raffles are not going to spark enthusiasm. Challenge and adventure will. That someone has sacrificed time, energy and comfort to help a cause that they felt strongly about is inspirational to children. If you are enthusiastic about

"Teachers have to find original ways of raising awareness of social and political issues amongst their pupils, because it is not something that most students find immediatey engaging. Similarly, voluntary work and fundraising generally have a poor image among young peer groups. Both of these factors make awareness presentations invaluable. Their passion is infectious and their commitment to their cause is inspirational. I have been to three or four such talks and the pupils are always buzzing with excitement in their wake."

Stuart Clayton, Teacher, Oundle School

spreading the word as far as possible and trying to inspire others, then this can be the most rewarding and effective element of the whole project.

- Participants' old schools - No matter how dreadful your relationships were with your teachers, they will be grateful for your giving time to the children!
- Local schools – The relevant people can be contacted through your Local Education Authority
- National Tour – This demands a lot of time and commitment, but ultimately not that difficult to organise. Contacts can be obtained from the relevant Local Education Authorities.
- Schools on your route – If you are considering some visits to international schools then this is worth pursuing for practical and emotional reasons. They may offer you some simple hospitality and they will almost certainly give you a big motivational boost with their enthusiasm.

Colleges and Universities

Through addressing higher education audiences you would be addressing the social group that makes more ethical and socially responsible decisions than any other. Colleges and universities also all have charity or RAG programmes, sometimes raising and donating hundreds of thousands of pounds. Obviously your first target would be the old university or college of the participants, which makes contacts easier to make and interest more straightforward to develop. There may even be specific funds annually awarded to charitable projects of the institution's alumni. Beyond this, it is merely a question of getting in touch with charity, NUS, events or society representatives and finding out what the possibilities are. Once you have made the initial effort to gain some kind of recognition at an institution, all the avenues for exploring its charity resources also become more apparent.

Organisations, associations and clubs

The list of groups that host speakers on worthwhile and interesting issues is endless and there is no reason why you should not target those who have the most to offer you, either in terms of direct support or the indirect accumulation of contacts. Similarly, as with the rest of the awareness and fundraising events that you are planning, organise appointments with community groups that fit in with a schedule designed to maximise exposure and impact. Each of these groups has a niche and a following, which may support a local publication and another opportunity for media coverage. When approaching such groups, it is best to stick to those within the communities of the members of the challenge team and to start with those most relevant to the individual, the cause or the means.

Top Tips for Presentations and Lectures

- Prepare thoroughly - Start by writing out your speech in full and editing it like a piece of prose. Then gradually reduce it until you can be prompted by a few words on some cards. This will help you have structure.

- Concentrate on 2-4 main points and introduce them clearly

- Follow the teacher's rule: tell them what you are about to say; say it; tell them what you have said.

- Make presentations relatively short, varied and exciting, changing the focus as often as possible and taking your audience through a range of emotions.

- Use different media to communicate – photos, video and audio clips all help convey the excitement of your project.

- Consider using PowerPoint - It can be very useful for emphasising your key messages and giving the presentation structure. However, don't fall into the following common traps:
  - Distracting yourself and your audience from an exciting topic with drab or tacky slides
  - Overcomplicating the slides – avoid too much text and too many styles and gimmicks
  - Relying on PowerPoint – you need to convey your enthusiasm for using passion and intensity.

- Offer lots of opportunities for your audience to follow up their interest – once you have them hooked, keep hold of them.

- Be Confident – What you have done is an inspiration.

In 1997 Sue and Victoria Riches became part of the first all female expedition to the North Pole. Since returning, the mother daughter team began a remarkable series of lectures, school and business presentations and after-dinner speeches, using their intense polar experience as a means of inspiring hundreds of audiences across the country.

Getting Involved with the Cause

At the core of a charity challenge is the impact on a particular cause. This is also its most potent reward. Many people miss out on what can be the most worthwhile legacy of taking on a challenge. If you have put the decision about which charity you will support first you will have personal motives for doing this. If the charity has been a late addition or simply a means to getting a place in an event then there is even more reason to foster a relationship. For the success of the challenge, the personal benefits, your work as a fundraiser and in raising awareness, getting involved with the cause is essential. And there are so many ways to do it…

Understanding

A good knowledge of your charity's work and its impact is very easy to achieve. Page 128 helps you get together the tools for raising awareness. Make your way from the human stories at the heart of their work to the broad social and political issues that surround it.

Project Visits

Nothing can replace witnessing the work of charities first-hand and meeting the people whose lives are changed by it. Realising that you are a part of these changes is immensely rewarding and will make every aspect of your challenge more exciting and emotive.

- **As part of the challenge** – If you are planning a challenge independently then you have every opportunity to intertwine it with the cause through project visits. Your route could take you from one site to the next for example. Many charities and operators now offer the chance to visit projects en route during international expeditions.
- **Beyond the challenge** – Many challenges do not incorporate project visits into the event, but this does not mean that they cannot be organised. Contact your charity about the possibility of visiting a project or service either before or after the challenge.

When approaching your charity's head office or contacting its projects and services be aware of their limited time and resources. More often than not, supporters are welcomed warmly, but it may take time to organise or simply not be possible. There are also charities whose sensitive work is not suited to lots of observers.

ActionAid, the international development agency, work with their participants, in both organised and independent challenges, to help them get a better understanding of their worldwide fight against poverty. Those taking part in ActionAid challenges are able to visit one of the local projects and meet some of those helped by their fundraising work. ActionAid challenge participants come away from these project visits feeling humbled and inspired by the stories of the people they meet, and the difference they have helped achieve. These visits are usually classed as the highlight of the event.

As part of their independent challenge, "Mission Malawi" for ActionAid, the team of 10 cyclists made their way from Lilongwe to Mzuzu where they met with children at the St. John's Orphanage Project. Here ActionAid provides a home for children orphaned by HIV/AIDS, and funds skills-based vocational training for teenage orphans, helping them to set up a living for themselves and their families. Read their profile on page 38.

Participants in ActionAid's Inca Trail Trek meet children at a school in Paucarcoto. The school in this poor village on the outskirts of Cusco receives support from ActionAid in the form of teacher training, educational materials and, recently, the first ever computers to arrive in the village.

Volunteering

A challenge fundraising project is, essentially, voluntary work, as it involves giving up your time and effort as a means of contributing to a cause. But there is another element that can be added to your project that makes the whole undertaking even more worthwhile and constructive, as well as more attractive to potential supporters. Beyond raising funds and awareness for your chosen cause or causes, consider spending time working as a volunteer in a particular project either connected to your charity or, on an international challenge, to the area through which you are travelling.

The benefits of introducing this aspect to your project, or becoming part of an organised challenge event that includes such work, are many.

- You will be able to connect much more closely with your cause and gain a greater understanding of its impact
- By volunteering for a project in host countries you show a real interest in their land and their lives and will be rewarded with closer relationships
- The more your project includes a willingness to engage directly with the its cause the more credibility you have with potential supporters
- A period of voluntary work is a perfect way to expand upon the relationship within your project between the cause and the route
- As a means of ending, beginning or dividing up a challenge, it gives the whole project much more definition
- You can use your challenge as a way of helping you to raise funds for supporting your voluntary work, although you should make as much of a contribution as you can
- Your awareness work will take on a whole new dimension due to the experiences and resources that volunteering work makes available to you

What kind of work?

There are hundreds of options for voluntary work and the best thing to do is have a look at some of the resources suggested in the reference section. Voluntary work could range from a day of reading to children at a local hospital leading up to a marathon challenge, to a six month position in a developing country having cycled 5,000 miles to get there. Whatever you include, it will give your project an ideal additional asset.

Voluntary work is often immensely rewarding and even if you have never considered it your 'kind of thing', now is the time to start thinking a little differently. You have made a decision to do something amazing by raising funds and awareness for charity, so take a step further and you will certainly not regret it.

➤➤ In 2004, Colin Brooks cycled through South America to raise money for ActionAid and undertook volunteering work as a photographer as part of the challenge.

"Even though the cycling expedition was an essential part of my project, looking back, it was my time volunteering as a photographer that has really left the greatest impression on me, and I highly recommend anyone thinking of doing a similar charity challenge to consider volunteering their skills or time in some way, to really experience life in the part of the world they travel to. My volunteer work has really given me an understanding of ActionAid's work and of daily life in the high Andes, and through my challenge I have gotten to know Bolivia and Peru in a way I never would have been able to as a tourist.

I returned to Britain with a new sense of direction in life that had previously been unfamiliar, determined to establish myself as a professional photojournalist and to continue raising awareness of developing world issues. I put together an exhibition of photography from my project, which has been exhibited on Peruvian national television, and in La Paz, Spain and London. Through the exhibition, my project has continued to raise funds and gain publicity for ActionAid even though I'm no longer pedalling across the Andes."

Colin Brooks

➤➤ Andy Shackleton volunteered with the British Executive Services Overseas in Ethiopia in 2004 and on his return used a charity challenge to raise money for some of the communities he had worked with.

"Early retirement found me in the privileged position of being in charge of my own schedules for the first time in my life. I visited a volunteering exhibition in Manchester and came across an organisation called BESO - the British Executive Services Overseas. I had spent 30 years teaching all things practical to secondary school students, which gave me skills that they valued and therefore a successful membership application. Then came the phone call in January 2004. Within weeks, I was facing one of the biggest challenges of my life. My time with BESO in Ethiopia was a near-vertical learning curve at times.

Based on the urban regions of Addis Ababa, Bahir Dar and Harar, my specific remit lay with the handicraft industry - its strengths, weaknesses and opportunities for development. The one month programme embraced meetings with support agencies, visits to manufacturers, interviews with their owners and operatives and preparation of a lengthy report.

But having visited educational establishments in Ethiopia that simply do not have any books, I had to do something to help. On my return I ran the London Marathon to raise money for (huge) shipping costs to send books I collected from local schools. I raised a shade over £2,200, which has meant that, in addition to 100kg plus of recycled books, I can purchase some new ones too."

Andy Shackleton

Volunteering Challenges

The concept of a charity challenge extends to any kind of sacrifice of time and effort in return for support. This sacrifice can be very productively put to use in the form of sponsored volunteering. In recent years such an idea has become increasingly popular and this is a very positive trend that promises to give thousands more people opportunities to enjoy the experience of volunteering and also to invest millions more pounds in community projects around the world.

 Find a comprehensive list of volunteering challenge opprtunities on the website.

Orna O'Toole with her team-mates and new friends in Sri Lanka during her Community Challenge rebuilding project

In June 2005 Orna O'Toole travelled to Sri Lanka to participate in a Community Challenge, run by tour operator Charity Challenge and International housing charity Habitat for Humanity. The construction project contributed to the rebuilding process in the wake of the devastating Asian Tsunami of December 2004.

"I was initially asked to participate in the challenge through work. The idea was to raise the profile of women in the building industry and as I work for the National House Building Council as an environmental engineer it was ideal. After being briefed about the situation in Sri Lanka by Habitat for Humanity we were itching to get started.

Physically, I coped well, I am fairly fit and the heat wasn't too much of a problem as long as we kept drinking water. Emotionally, there were so many things that had a huge affect on me: remembering why the house had to be built in the first place and seeing the faces of the family that would live there working along side you; remembering that it wasn't a normal construction site - we were there to re-build a home as part of a community; seeing how little the family had left after the Tsunami and how strong they were to continue rebuilding their lives; leaving every day to go back to a hotel and seeing the smiles on their faces every morning when we turned up to site.

The experience made me re-align what I consider important - we worry about material things which make life more complex than it needs to be. The families in Sri Lanka are content that they have their lives and the lives of their dear ones - a house is a bonus."

Orna O'Toole

Physical
Challenge

At the very heart of your charity challenge is the test of physical endurance. This is where you show your grit, where you surprise yourself. It is in the depths of exhaustion and the achievement of coming through it that you earn the right to ask people to support your cause. There is no choice but to be prepared. Your physical sacrifices do not just start and end with your challenge, but begin the moment you decide to take on a test of endurance.

This section tackles and simplifies the complex areas of conditioning, nutrition and health, and it draws on the know-how of our two physical challenge experts:

Physical Conditioning:

James Gero, Sports Medicine and Performance Enterprises

Nutrition:

Kathryn Bystany, Corpotential Limited

Physical Conditioning

Training and preparing physically for a charity challenge should not be intimidating. In fact, you should look forward to it, even if it is the first time that you have attempted anything like this. However, when setting a challenge that will force your body beyond its comfort zone, you have to be prepared physically and mentally for what that entails. Being blasé about health and fitness will set you up for a massive shock when you start and this applies to every kind of challenge. If your project is a short one then you may feel that you can get through it without too much preparation. If you are planning to take on a long project, then it might seem feasible to gradually acclimatise and adjust over the first few days and weeks. Both have been tried many times before and both have led to injury and failure. Your body and mind will quickly and painfully let you know if you have not prepared properly.

Why Do You Need to Train?

Physically

Think of the principle of evolution. Very slowly and gradually, human beings have developed in reaction to a chain of tiny changes in their surroundings, needs and demands. Physical conditioning follows exactly the same principle. Your body can only adapt physically at a relatively slow and gradual pace and will do so effectively in reaction to small and measured changes in the level of demands placed upon it. Too much change and your body will be out of its depth and rebel with pain and injuries. You simply cannot ask your body to do something that it has no experience of, because it will not be able to.

In the short-term, you are putting your ability to complete or continue a challenge at risk if you have to try and shock your body into surviving the physical trials. In the long-term, you risk causing injury that might have serious consequences for your health.

Mentally

Charity challenges are hard work and demand some real grit and determination, but ultimately they are meant to be rewarding and exciting. The degree to which this is so depends upon your level of physical preparation. Whatever the distance, the intensity or the length of your challenge, your personal perspective of it is crucial to your performance and success. This means that 2 hours of running can be as hard to break down into manageable chunks as three months of walking or cycling. So at the end of that twenty minutes or opening day you will struggle to imagine yourself ever finishing if you have been badly affected by the exertion. Worse, if you fail to complete a challenge because you have not prepared physically then you will always regret not committing more time to training.

On a Long-Term Challenge

There are so many elements of a long-term challenge that need attention and adaptation. The last thing you want is to

"Taking your physical preparation for the challenge seriously will play a major part in how much enjoyment and satisfaction you derive from it. Charity challenges are designed to be tough physical experiences, so a full training programme is crucial. Train consistently over time and don't wait until a month before the challenge to start training - so start now!"

Julie Thomas, Operations Manager, Across the Divide

be occupied by a hard mental battle of coming to terms with the physical tests ahead. Apart from the complete change in lifestyle to a predominantly physical one, you will also take on a routine that is at least partly foreign. However thoroughly you prepare, there will still be facets of your particular project that are unpredictable, and of course adjusting to these is one of the most rewarding parts of the challenge. This new routine may just involve organising youth hostel accommodation in the Lake District or finding your way across an ordinance survey map, or it may be a total transformation, demanding communicating in a new language and setting up camp in a jungle. Either way, dealing with cultural changes can be draining and bewildering, even for very resilient people. You will also be relying emotionally and organisationally on the rest of the group, or maybe completely by yourself for the first time. Being with people under intense physical and mental stress for the first time puts a lot of pressure on relationships. The more predictable that physical stress, the

more easily you will be able to adapt to each other and compromise. The less worry caused by the prospect of daily running, cycling, walking or swimming, the more quickly you will get into a comfortable routine. This demands a thorough physical preparation in the months leading up to the challenge.

On an international expedition you also have to deal with acclimatisation. Health issues concern any traveller, but daily exertion puts extra pressure on your ability to stay healthy. Your body will most likely react to different types of water, food, climates, altitude, new drugs, a shifted sleep pattern and everything else a new environment throws at it. However, arriving at your challenge well prepared is an essential ingredient of your performance.

"Throughout the physical conditioning process dig deep to find out why you are doing this challenge, it may be as simple as the fact that when you think of it, it makes you happy. The next stage is to hold that dream close to your heart. If your chips are down, and training has not gone to plan, think of it as an experience and just as a child learns to walk, falling over constantly, he does not look at its failure and start to worry but adheres to the fact that it is just a process of learning, enjoys that learning experience with the inner knowledge that one day there will be success. If during your training you feel that you set out to train at a certain distance or pace and have not succeeded, do not give up, evaluate and try again. Keep continuing to focus on that goal, that dream."

James Gero, **Sports Medicine and Performance Enterprises**

Challenge Training's

Everyone reading this will be embarking on challenges that vary enormously in length and difficulty, just as their levels of fitness will be very different. Beneficial to everyone about to undertake training for a physical endurance challenge are the principles of training. No matter what you aim to achieve, you should prepare as well as your time and resources allow. This involves getting the maximum benefits from each training session, each week and each month, as well as protecting your health.

1. Plan and Monitor

- Set short-term and long-term goals that correspond to the level of physical conditioning that you want to reach.
- Make a training schedule that suits you, your aims and your commitments.
- Monitor your progress regularly, including how you felt after each session.

2. Be Regular

- Put together a realistic training schedule that will allow you to build your fitness and strength gradually and consistently, and stick to it.
- Avoid crash training at all costs, as you will risk your health and most likely diminish your performance.

3. Warm Up and Warm Down

- At the beginning of every session, spend 5-10 minutes doing light exercise and then stretch thoroughly.
- Warming down is equally vital as it increases the blood flow to muscles which helps flush out the by-products of exercise, such as lactic acid.

4. Be Specific

- Your fitness and strength training should reflect your challenge – this is called specificity
- The closer you get to the event, the more this should be true.

5. Value Quality over Quantity

- The right type of training, for the right length of time and at the right intensity is far better than huge distances, heavy weights or long sessions.

Ten Commandments

6. Adapt Gradually and Sensibly

- Your body improves its physical capacity as a result of measured "overloading" i.e. when it is put under greater stress than it is used to.
- BUT increase your training workloads slowly and deliberately by no more than 10% a week.

7. Rest, Recover, Drink and Eat

- If you progress as a result of overloading then this progression takes place during the rest period. No rest and recovery = no progress.
- Include 'active recovery' sessions the day after hard training.
- Make your diet a priority and drink lots of fluids.
- Aim for 8 hours sleep, but more importantly maintain a regular sleep pattern.

8. Listen to Your Body

- If you are exhausted or in pain then your body is telling you to stop and rest.
- Make sure that it is your body and not your mind!

9. Work on Your Technique

- Endless training in the wrong way will slow your progress and cause injury.
- Get expert advice on your technique, even if you have been running, cycling or swimming for years.

10. Enjoy It!

- The training process should be something that you enjoy. There will be many moments of forcing yourself to train, but make sure that it does not become a total chore so do as much as you can to make it more fun: listen to music, find a training partner or group, buy a heart rate monitor and graph your progress, give your self treats and reward yourself

Training Methods

There are an enormous number of training methods out there and even then these will need to be adapted to suit the individual needs and demands of the challenge, the time available you have for training sessions and your own physical condition. Ultimately, you will be concentrating on two main areas of training – cardiovascular development (fitness) and muscular development (strength). These sessions can then be fitted into a schedule working backwards from your challenge. This will be explained in detail in the Planning and Monitoring section, starting on page 156.

FITNESS

Despite the variety of events, most endurance challenges, done for primarily charitable rather than competitive reasons, demand a certain type of fitness. In lay terms: you are aiming to do a relatively small amount of stuff for a long period of time, rather than a lot of stuff for a short period of time. In scientific terms, you will be aiming to increase the capacity of your cardiovascular system through aerobic, rather than anaerobic, exercise.

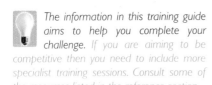
The information in this training guide aims to help you complete your challenge. If you are aiming to be competitive then you need to include more specialist training sessions. Consult some of the resources listed in the reference section.

For all challenges you need to increase your aerobic fitness and this is done by increasing your heart rate to a certain level for a certain period of time. Having done this, your body will adapt, during rest periods, to the demands that you have put on it and gradually you will be able to increase these demands until you reach the required level of fitness.

Heart Rate

Your heart rate (HR) can be compared to a rev counter in a car. If it is too low then you stall and make no progress. If it is too high then you risk damage. To take the analogy a step further, every time you increase your aerobic capacity you gain another gear: the revs stay the same but your speed increases, or you can maintain the same speed at fewer revs.

As we do not have in-built rev counters, then it is a good idea to buy a heart rate monitor. This will allow you to train in a very controlled way, giving your body the exact workout it needs. Furthermore, you will be able to monitor your progress. If your resources do not allow this, or you just have not got round to it yet, then there are two ways in which you can stay in control of your heart rate. Firstly, listen to your body. As will be explained, most of your training will be done at Low Intensity, i.e. between 60 and 85% of your maximum heart rate. At this level, you should be able to hold a conversation and should not be gasping for breath. Or you can check your pulse whenever you need to and count the beats per minute. This is not especially convenient during exercise and actually pretty difficult to do, but through the difference between your resting rate and that at the very end of exercise you can gauge your progress.

Resting Heart Rate

To work out your training levels you first need to measure your resting heart rate. This is best done first thing in the morning and preferably over a week, with an average taken at the end. Make sure you are totally relaxed – if your alarm has just gone off and you are dying for that first trip to the bathroom, then your heart rate will be slightly elevated. Count beats per minute on your wrist or neck (not with your thumb) and write it down.

Max Heart Rate

To work out an approximate maximum heart rate, from which you can then calculate your training range, you can simply deduct your age from 220. So if you are 30 years old, then you have a maximum heart rate of 190. Low Intensity training would be done at between 114 and 162 beats per minute.

However, this method does not take into account the size of your heart, which could considerably affect this figure, and is only accurate to approximately 60% of the population. So, unless you have access to a proper lab test, then get your trainers on and work it out on your own.

Calculating heart rate

- Warm up for 10-15 minutes, with a combination of light exercise and stretching
- Workout at near maximum effort for 4-6 minutes
- Complete the last 1-2 minutes (after the 4-6) at absolute max
- Read highest HR from monitor or do count straight after exercise
- BE CAREFUL
  - This can only be done by people who are accustomed to this level of exertion – not for those new to training.
  - If you have any health problems, particularly cardiovascular, then consult your doctor before doing this.

Karvonen Formula

With these two figures you can use the Karvonen formula to work out what your target heart rate should be for certain types of training.

(Max HR – Resting HR) x intensity (%) + Resting HR

John has a resting HR of 65 and a max HR of 195 and he is planning to train at around 75%.

$(195 - 65)$ x $0.75 + 65 = 162.5$
So, John would aim to reach and maintain a heart rate of 162-163 bpm during his session.

Training Levels

There are essentially four levels of cardiovascular training which perform different roles within your physical conditioning. These levels are divided using their corresponding target heart rate.

Heart rates

Active Recovery (AR) 50-65% range

- This range is not used to increase your cardiovascular capacity, but instead to maximise the benefits of your recovery. The increased blood flow helps clear the muscles of by-products from more intense CV workouts, as well as improve the body's ability to exercise regularly, without involving any overload.

Low Intensity 60-85% range

- Low Intensity training will give you basic aerobic fitness and muscular conditioning and also improve your body's ability to break down fat and use it as an energy source. The type of training is predominantly long at a moderate pace. At the low end of this range you should be able to maintain a conversation with ease, at the high end with moderate difficulty.

Sub-maximal Intensity 85-95%

- This level of training improves your overall endurance and fitness by increasing your "anaerobic threshold", which is the point at which (in fact it is more of transition "grey area" than a point) you begin to stop being able to provide oxygen quickly enough to your muscles and start to power them anaerobically. This would be applicable for a challenge that will demand a variety of levels of exertion, some of which are very intense.

High Intensity 95-100%

- High intensity training improves your sprinting ability. Unless you aim to be seriously competitive you will not need to operate at this maximum output when your energy demands exceed your aerobic metabolism (your ability to provide oxygen to your muscles). When this takes place you exercise without oxygen, in which your body can do without generating lactic acid for a certain period of time, normally 10-20 seconds (the anaerobic alactic period). After this time, lactic acid is produced as a by-product, and this can be sustained for between 10 seconds and, in exceptional athletes, 2-3 minutes (the anaerobic lactic period).

Training Sessions

Linked to each of the levels of cardiovascular training are different types of session. These will give you the tools with which you can create a schedule that suits your needs and demands. The Planning and Monitoring section will give you more information about exactly how to do this.

Heart Rate Maintenance Sessions

These steady-state, sessions will make up the vast majority of endurance challenge sessions. These should be done for a minimum of 30 minutes and a maximum, for long sessions, of about 2 hours (15-20 miles running, for example) and should be the main part of your thoroughly planned and monitored training schedule to maximise progress and maintain health.

There are essentially 3 types of HR maintenance sessions:

50-60% - This level of exertion over a period of at least 2 months is recommended for absolute beginners in order to adapt to physical activity.

60-70% - Having become used to regular physical activity through adaptation sessions, your base cardiovascular training should be done at this level.

70-80% - Having established a foundation to your fitness over a period of 4-6 months for the beginner, these sessions will take your cardiovascular capacity to the next level

Where you aim to maintain your HR within this range will depend upon:
• Your base fitness levels
• The stage of your training programme
• Your ambition in terms of pace for the challenge

• Your target intensity (easy/hard) for that particular session

Interval Sessions

Intervals, i.e. specific and relatively short periods of intense exercise and recovery are a great way to vary your training and improve your cardiovascular capacity. Depending upon your goals for the challenge and the time with which you have to prepare, interval sessions can be a very useful part of training. The means of progressing is by increasing the period of intense exertion and decreasing the rest period.

During interval sessions you will be aiming to hit Sub-maximal Intensity (85-95%) during the exercise period, and aim

• A solid base of fitness is required before interval training becomes an option within your schedule.
• Watch your HR carefully throughout interval training.
• If your primary aim is to complete the challenge, then do not include interval sessions to the detriment of steady-state endurance workouts.
• Interval sessions should be shorter than your HR maintenance workouts

to keep HR above 50% of max during the rest periods. This will maximise the endurance and recovery benefits.

Interval Variations

- Time – set predetermined work and recovery interval times, normally 2-8 minutes for work and usually 60-90 seconds recovery.

- Distance – set a distance that will take at most about 3 minutes at high intensity, and a recovery distance of roughly half that. Distance could be replaced by elevation.

- Pyramids – this involves gradually increasing and then decreasing the length of the intervals. For example, on a rowing machine, 1 hard stroke, one easy stroke; 2 hard, 2 easy, etc. On a run, 10 hard strides/seconds, 10 easy etc.

- Short Repeats – these focus on increasing speed and involve short 90-100% effort intervals followed by longer rest intervals. Improvement comes as the length of these intervals converge.

- Fartleks – this Swedish term describes bursts of speed and these interval sessions are great fun and ideal for a number of training situations. Basically, the length, distance and recovery time are completely up to you, as is the direction, form and exercise. For running, try high stepping, clipping your bottom with your heels, or running backwards, and introduce push ups, crunches or walking lunges in the recovery interval.

- Indian Running – these are ideal for group training, in either running, hiking or cycling. The group spreads out into single file, then the back marker speeds up to overtake the group and hit the front, at which point the new rear marker does the same.

Active Recovery Sessions

These sessions can help your body recover the day after hard training and also develop your ability to endure repeated and long term physical exertion. If you wake up feeling stiff and sore 24 or 48 hours after training, then rather than wait 3 or four days for it to subside you can accelerate recovery by undertaking very light exercise. They involve very low intensity non/low impact exercise, such as swimming, cycling or walking and are complemented very well by yoga or static stretching work, lasting anywhere between 30 minutes and an hour in total. Aim to maintain your HR between 50-60% of maximum – these sessions do not aim to increase your cardiovascular capacity but instead aid recovery and help acclimatise your body to exercise. These are a great opportunity to try different sports and disciplines. For a runner who has one main long run a week, an active recovery session of gentle swimming or cycling scheduled the day afterwards is ideal.

"Active rest gives you time to rebuild and regenerate the mind and body. Don't spend it abusing your body. It is about recharging the batteries, possibly going to bed earlier. It is a good time to look over the training log, re-evaluate your progress, and gain inspiration from where you have come from and where this journey is taking you. Have fun and come back to your training schedule hungry for more.

Great active recovery sessions can be something like windsurfing, swimming or another totally different sport to your main challenge activity. Much of the benefits are in the mental recuperation these offer. "

James Gero, **Sports Medicine and Performance Enterprises**

STRENGTH

Cardiovascular training improves your body's efficiency in converting oxygen into red blood cells and distributing these cells to your muscles. Resistance training increases the strength and endurance of these muscles. To complete a tough endurance challenge you will benefit enormously from increased muscular strength through resistance training.

The main principle behind this type of training is very similar to that which guides cardiovascular work: by overloading your muscles and placing them under greater stress through resistance than they are used to, they will respond by increasing their capacity, with the aid of rest and nutrition. The type of resistance training that you undertake will dictate the type of capacity that they develop.

There are many debates surrounding muscular conditioning, its benefits and its techniques, however very few of them can be addressed in detail here. A range of excellent and detailed manuals for strength training are available and some of them are listed in the reference section, so if you do want more information head to the library or the book shop. Similarly, if you decide to include weight training in your schedule then you should seek the advice of a strength coach in compiling a programme specific to your needs and ambitions.

Potential Advantages

- Increased muscle strength, improving your power and speed

- Increased muscular endurance and stamina, enabling you to continue performing well for a longer period of time

- Improved co-ordination and balance, which increases your efficiency

- Reduced likelihood of injuries as muscles, tendons and ligaments become more resilient, as well as improved bone health.

Potential Concerns

- Increased body mass can make you less efficient in your chosen discipline.

  - Increased weight to carry and stress on joints for high impact disciplines
  - Possible increased burden upon the heart, which works harder to pump blood to deliver oxygen to bigger muscles
  - Potential decrease in flexibility due to muscle bulk

- Over emphasis on resistance training will be detrimental to your cardiovascular progress

Types of Strength Training

The issue of cause and effect within resistance training is very complex. However, for the purposes of amateur training and charity challenge projects, there are essentially two types of resistance training. Despite the large grey areas, dividing this training into two has the advantage of demonstrating to the challenger what sessions are most appropriate to include in their schedule.

- **High Weight/Low Repetitions** = muscular capacity/power + size

- **Low Weight/High Repetitions** = muscular endurance/stamina + definition

 Use strength sessions as a way of addressing the specific physical demands of your challenge and it will be an important asset to your conditioning.

For the purposes of most endurance challenges, you will not be aiming to pile on muscle mass. Most participants will be performing the same action repeatedly and the output of each action will very rarely be over around 60-70% of your maximum muscle power, and most of the time far less than this.

A general guide is to aim to complete 2-3 sets of 10-15 repetitions at around 60% of your maximum weight. By the final couple of reps of each set you should be struggling to complete the lift/exercise.

Weight Training Basics

Here are a number of guidelines that will help make the most out of your weight training:

- Set Relevant Goals - This is true of all your training, but easily forgotten when it comes to lifting weights or undertaking resistance work. Set goals that are specific to your overall aim – completing the challenge.

- Be Balanced - Muscular imbalance increases your chances of overuse injuries, so make sure that you balance strength work within and between muscle groups.

- Use Your Own Body Weight - Good weight lifting is about balance and this also applies to the relationship between body weight and strength. Managing your own weight is an excellent target. For example, if you aim to increase upper body strength then you can measure your progress against improvements in press-ups, pull ups and sit-ups, rather than kilograms lifted or pushed. For lower body exercises, keep in mind how much weight you will be carrying during the challenge and use that as a guideline.

- Use Free Weights - Dumbbells and barbells may seem more suited to bodybuilders and pro athletes, but this is not the case. Free weights, as opposed to machines, give you the benefits of increasing the strength of specific muscles as well as the surrounding stabilising muscles, producing more balanced results. If you have never used free-weights before then consult a qualified expert.

- Be Controlled - **Perform resistance work slowly and deliberately. This applies to both halves of the exercise.**

- Concentrate On Your Form - **Far too often form and technique are sacrificed for increased weight or repetitions. By doing this you risk injury and undermine the benefits of those repetitions. If you are trying an exercise for the first time, practise the movements with a very low and manageable weight or no weight at all.**

- Breath - **Maintain your breathing pattern when you are lifting weights. Aim to breath out on the push/lift and in on the lowering of the weight.**

- Vary Your Routine - **It is very easy to get bored by performing the same sets of exercises in the gym, so regularly change exercises.**

- Above All BE SAFE - **Weight training is potentially dangerous and you risk trauma and overuse injuries by not undertaking it sensibly: get expert advice on your programme; train with a partner; only lift weights that you are comfortable with; check your equipment thoroughly; wear appropriate and non-baggy clothing.**

Circuit Training

This is a great means of getting the best of both worlds: increasing muscular strength and endurance as well as giving your cardiovascular system a good workout. For a circuit training session you should aim to be completing a circuit of between 6 to 12/14 exercises for between 30 and 60 seconds each. After each exercise you move directly onto the next one. This circuit should be completed between 2 and 4 times, with rest intervals of between 3 and 5 minutes between circuits. Circuit training is ideal for a group of people and you can also join up to a class that makes them focussed, structured and fun.

"If you want to build upper body muscles, you need to lift and lower the weight extremely slowly. This creates the tension needed to work the muscles hard every inch of the way. Spend six seconds lifting the weight, then six seconds lowering it, pausing once at the top of the move."

Jonathan Lewis, Balance Performance Physiotherapy

Planning Your Training

You are all preparing for a variety of challenges with different needs and demands. Everyone has a history of health and fitness that is very individual. Putting these ambitions and issues into categories is dangerous and risks giving people training programmes to which they are ill-suited. Consequently, this section aims to give you the fundamental principles of planning and monitoring. No matter what kind of advice you receive from those who know and understand your own needs, they will not be able to accompany you every step of the way, so such principles will help you plan and monitor you own training and prepare safely and efficiently for the challenge ahead.

For a tailor-made programme there are a number of options, which are examined on pages 148-152. These represent the best ways of making sure that your programme is appropriate.

A Training Schedule

A schedule is vital to your physical preparation and ensures success, because you will know exactly where you have been and where you are going. Your progress becomes tangible and quantifiable, instead of mysterious and unpredictable.

Principle 1: The Road Ahead

Visualise a road. You are standing at Point A and you want to get to the end of the road, Point B. How long this road is depends upon your current condition and the demands of your challenge, and is also determined by the basic rule of thumb for all physical conditioning: do not increase your training load by more than 10% a week. Your path along this road needs to be smooth and gradual - cutting corners will only reduce your chances of success and increase the risk of injury.

Principle 2 : Establishing Point A and Point B

Point A

Establishing your current physical condition relies upon a knowledge and understanding of the following factors:

- **Your fitness and strength levels**
This can be established through a number of different tests or can simply be measured in terms of the most strenuous physical activity that you currently perform regularly, whether this is running 8 miles in an hour or walking for 30 minutes.

In very basic terms, you will gradually increase and develop your training load from this level of activity to reach the level and nature of physical conditioning required for your challenge.

- **Your training history.**
Even if you currently exercise very little, your immediate training potential will be affected by your training history.

- **Your medical history**
The amount of stress that you can put on your body during the training process is also determined by any weaknesses in your health. Consult qualified professionals about how your medical history may affect your training.

Point B

Examine the physical needs and demands of your challenge carefully. These main areas need considering:
- The distance of the challenge
- Your target time and therefore pace
- The terrain you will be covering
- The conditions of the challenge (weather, altitude etc.)
- Your equipment and its demands

Principle 3: Training Phases

This road between Point A and Point B ahead needs dividing up into sections which are called phases. They are designed to ensure that every aspect of your physical conditioning is given sufficient attention.

1. General Phase

This phase makes up around half of the training period (usually between 3-5 months within a training period that targets one major event/challenge), and consists of improving your general physical endurance levels by gradually increasing the volume of your training. It is an excellent time to develop good training skills, such as correct lifting techniques for strength training or incorporating a body strength programme. Introduce plenty of variety to your schedule during this phase, such

as circuit training or aqua fitness. Locate the weaknesses, sort out nutritional habits and mentally prepare yourself for the demands of the challenge.

2. Transitional phase

This is a good Active Recovery phase, normally lasting 1-2 weeks before embarking on the Specific phase. You are aiming to recuperate without losing your hard work. Have massages, osteopathy or physiotherapy to locate dysfunctional areas and weaknesses. Enjoy the family and re-focus on the goal. Good time to work on, meditation, yoga, stretching.

3. Specific Phase

This phase normally lasts from anywhere between 6-12 weeks. This phase aims to closely replicate that which is to be endured on the challenge. If you are running a 100 miler, it does not mean that during your training sessiong you have to run 50-80 miles or a marathon if you are training for a marathon. However, you may spend 4 hours running up stadium stairs to simulate running the canyons, or for example run on the beach to simulate the sand in the desert. In this phase the goal is to replicate the activity required for the challenge.

4. Pre-Challenge Phase

This, commonly known as the pre-competition phase. It normally lasts for 3-6 weeks and is about maintenance, recuperation, ironing out any of the problems that still exist, keeping the training very specific and increasing the intensity of volume which will be exhibited during the challenge.

The final 2-3 weeks of this final phase involves tapering your training (see pages 146-147 for more details).

A Helping Hand...

This section is designed to give you a better understanding of the main principles that lie behind physical conditioning. However, the process of preparing for a charity challenge is essentially personal. Individuals progress in different ways and respond to different stimuli. Similarly, you will undoubtedly encounter problems and need specific questions addressing. The first place to look for such advice and expertise is at your local gym, which you may already be a member of or will be planning to join.

Nick Hudson, an Academy Trainer at Holmes Place shares his experience of helping thousands of charity challenge participants.

What can a gym offer a charity challenge participant?

Putting together a schedule for the challenge

We can break down the seemingly huge event ahead into smaller, more manageable segments (you will sometimes hear this called "perodisation"). This will enable you to gradually build your fitness levels up to where they need to be without becoming overwhelmed.

Form and technique

We will check your form and technique while you train for your challenge to improve efficiency of movement, and even more importantly to minimise the risk of injury which is an ever-present concern when taxing the body beyond its normal "functional capacity."

Monitoring and assessment

We recognise that it is important to "chunk down" any large goal into smaller, more manageable segments. This will ensure your success, not just from a physiological, but also a psychological point of view, as you will be able to view the training for the challenge as a series of mini-challenges rather than one big one. By so doing we can check your progress at agreed stages along the way

Health and injury

When attempting a challenge, it can be easy to leave your training until the last minute (and risk not completing the event or worse still getting injured during the challenge through being underprepared). It is equally possible to actually overtrain and get injured before the event itself. We can assess the volume of training that is most appropriate for you to ensure your success.

Diet and nutrition

As most challenges are far more taxing on the body than our activities of daily living, you must consider paying more attention to your diet. What we can do is ensure your body is as well-fuelled as possible!

Cross training and classes

With dozens of different classes on offer, we can point you in the direction of a class/es that will be most beneficial for your challenge. The concept of "specificity" is very important (i.e. doing something that most closely mimics the challenge you are going to complete) so we will help you choose the class that most closely fits the bill!

Nick Hudson, Academy Trainer, **Holmes Place**

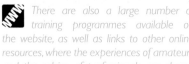 *There are also a large number of training programmes available on the website, as well as links to other online resources, where the experiences of amateurs and the advice of professionals are shared and analysed.*

If you want more personalised and full-time guidance then you should consider a personal trainer or consultant. These can be found in local listings or be recommended by your gym.

When selecting a coach/trainer, the best advice comes from those who have actively experienced challenges themselves. Although it is impossible for them to share the same experience, they will understand the ups and downs that are associated with training. As you aspire towards your challenge, you may well feel the need to be around those who are also aspiring. It is extremely difficult for a person to have knowledge of the difficulties that may present themselves and feel the shear elevation that you will be experiencing on your successful completion if they have never challenged themselves. Be patient and try to include those that are close to you as they may well want to be part of your experience. If you have particular training needs or want to prepare for some of the toughest challenges out there then an experienced coach can tailor your programme and draw a plan & monitor your progress around your event

James Gero, Sports Medicine and Performance Enterprises

NIck McConnell finishes the London Marathon for Childline within his target time of three hours thanks to a programme developed by a personal trainer.

Challenge Profile:

Riding the Silk Road for Merlin

Alexandra Tolstoy

Born 1973 – Writer and Traveller

The Challenge - Riding the Silk Road from Merv to Xian on horse and camel

Our route along the Silk Road covered five thousand miles through Central Asia and China. We became the first people to retrace this ancient trading route on horse and camel since the merchants of the Middle Ages.

The journey was the idea of Sophia Cunningham, one of our team members. She had studied Religion at university where we all met, and wrote her dissertation on the movement of Buddhism along the Silk Road, which inspired her to organise the expedition.

Our journey took us through some of the least-known and most beautiful regions of the world: Turkmenistan, Uzbekistan, Kyrgyzstan, the Taklamakan Desert and China, and the road we followed echoed with some of the mightiest names in history – Genghis Khan, Tamerlane and the nineteenth-century players of the Great Game of Empire between Britain and Russia.

The route took us 8 months to complete.

The Charity - Merlin

Merlin is the only specialist UK charity which responds worldwide with vital healthcare and medical relief for vulnerable people caught up in natural disasters, conflict, disease and health system collapse.

We chose this charity because we wanted to give something back to the peoples through whose lands we would be travelling and Merlin has fantastic tuberculosis projects in Uzbekistan. Although the expedition cost £80,000, none of this money came from funds we raised for Merlin, which came to £30,000.

We received a great deal of media coverage and my book on the journey, *The Last Secrets of the Silk Road*, helped raise the profile of the trip and awareness for the charity.

Fundraising Tip
Giving lectures on the trip can raise huge amounts of money and awareness. We gave lectures at the Royal Geographical Society, which raised the majority of our money for Merlin

Diary

"In spite of all the difficulties, this year of my life was without a doubt more exciting and rewarding than any other. We saw some of the most beautiful and dramatic landscapes on the planet, and met some of its most colourful and interesting people."

Best Moments

Riding through the remote valleys of the Tien Shan Mountains of Kyrgyzstan. The landscape must have looked the same to the players of the Great Game. It was in this romantic setting that I met my future husband – our horse guide.

Hardest Moments

Riding through the Taklamakan Desert was the hardest part of the trip. By this stage we were on camels and it was 45 – 50°C every day. We rose at 4.00am in order to avoid the midday heat and stopped riding at 12.00pm, when we lay in the sweltering shade of an open-sided tent, longing for darkness with its relative coolness. For more than two months we endured these horrific temperatures, only seeing trees and vegetation once every couple of weeks in tiny desert oases. We wondered desperately at times how we could continue and dreaded each morning.

Biggest Problem

Saddle sores on the horses and camels – the British are much more sentimental about animals than other nationalities and this caused friction.

Alexandra crossing the Taklamakan Desert by camel with her team

Nutrition and Fluids

1. Nutrition

By taking on an endurance challenge you are making serious demands upon your body and for these to be fulfilled it must be fuelled properly.

FOOD IS FUEL

Throughout the training process the right diet will maximise your progress and help prevent injury. During the challenge itself your success relies upon sustaining your performance over a certain period of time, so you have no choice but to give your body what it needs. The principles behind eating for exercise are in essence very simple, but you must make it a priority. When you finish a long training session you may want to reward yourself with a bag of crisps and a can of coke, but your system needs the required nutrients to bring the hard work to bear. On a challenge expedition, you may be exhausted at the end of a mammoth day, but you have to take on enough of the right foods to be able to get up and do the same thing the next day.

So the first rule of eating properly is give it time and thought. Establish a habit of shopping more carefully and preparing well-balanced meals during your training and preparation. Surrounding the challenge itself, make eating part of your planning. This could range from loading your body with the required levels of carbohydrates in the run up to a marathon to carrying adequate calories for three days of totally self-sufficient travelling. Remember:

- Training sessions are potentially wasted unless you give your body means of recovering, repairing and growing
- You will find exercise easier if you provide yourself with the right fuel
- You significantly reduce the chance of illness or injury by eating properly
- If you are fit and healthy then the right diet will enable you achieve anything

Eating for exercise

A great book by chef Michael Roux Jnr, The Marathon Chef – Food for Getting Fit, demonstrates that to eat the right diet for exercise does not have to involve cutting out everything you enjoy. He also makes the crucial point that within a routine that regularly makes physical demands of your body, it becomes more efficient at craving the right foods. So, listen to those cravings, but avoid foods that are high in sugar, high in salt or highly refined.

The main principles of eating for exercise are as follows:

- **Calorie output must at least be matched by calorie input. If it is not, then you burn fat, and if you have no fat reserves you start to burn muscle tissue.**
- **The average daily output is 2,000 for women and 2,500 for men. For every hour of exercise you can add between 200 and 500 calories to this total.**
- **Your diet should approximately consist of 55-65% carbohydrates, 15-25% proteins and 20-30% fats**
- **Eat as many wholemeal foods as possible**
- **Eat a lot of fresh fruit and vegetables (raw as often as possible)**

Think **Variety, Regularity and Colours**
- Try and have a least 6 different foods on your plate or in your sandwich (spices, herbs, olive oil, lemon juice and the like all count)
- Include lots of colourful foods in your meals (natural colours of course)
- Eat regularly: every 3 hours during periods of training

Kathryn Bistany, Corpotential Limited

Balance - Carbs, Protein and Fats

Carbohydrates

These are the main constituents of your diet and they should make up 50-60% of your diet, but equally importantly they need to be of the right kind. The Glycaemic Index (GI) has been used a lot recently to describe a type of weight loss diet. In fact it is an ideal guide for everyone. If food is fuel then you have to know what kind of fuel you are using and GI is a great way of doing this.

What it describes is the speed at which carbohydrates are converted into sugar by the body. The index itself relates to the amount by which 50 grams of a certain carbohydrate increases your blood sugar level in 2 hours as compared to pure glucose (GI 100). The GI is an ideal companion for your nutritional intake while preparing for and completing your challenge, as it allows you to control your energy levels and appetite very effectively.

High GI Carbohydrates

High GI food (70+) sharply increases your blood sugar levels, which triggers the release of insulin from the pancreas. The insulin removes excess glucose from the blood sugar levels, to maintain them at a normal level. However, a sustained intake of high GI foods causes excess insulin to be produced, which triggers the conversion of the glucose into fat. The short-term energy boost may potentially be followed by feeling sleepy and you will also find yourself feeling hungry soon afterwards. In the long term, you will put on excess weight.

High GI carbs are best eaten only before, during or after exercise, which will ensure your blood sugar levels are not depleted.

➤➤ High GI: white rice, potatoes, bread, shredded/puffed cereals, doughnuts, pancakes, white bread, almost all processed cereals, cakes, biscuits, crisps

Medium and Low GI Carbs

These carbohydrates should make up the bulk of your intake. They are absorbed more slowly into the body therefore providing a gradual release of energy. A meal of medium GI carbohydrates two or three hours before exercise will help sustain your energy levels.

The vast majority of fruit and vegetables are low/medium GI, with carrots, parsnips and pumpkin as the most common exceptions.

Remember that you can slightly lower the GI level of your meal by adding some lemon or vinegar

➤➤ Medium GI: bananas, honey, rye bread, basmati/wild rice, cous cous, new potatoes, pasta, granary bread, wholemeal bread, raisins, spinach, sweetcorn, muesli, mangoes, pineapple.

➤➤ Low GI: beans (except broad), peas, lentils, oatmeal porridge, high fibre cereals, broad/butter beans, chick peas, basmati rice, barley, bulgar wheat.

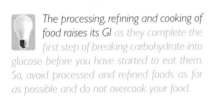

The processing, refining and cooking of food raises its GI as they complete the first step of breaking carbohydrate into glucose before you have started to eat them. So, avoid processed and refined foods as far as possible and do not overcook your food.

Carbo-loading

There are a number of theories on how best to maximise your performance during an event, but the current consensus is that you need to fully fuel yourself by loading on carbohydrates during the days leading up to an endurance event. The aim of this is to top up your body's glycogen stores. During this period you will also be tapering your training, so do not go over the top, as less training will provide your body with more carbohydrate for storage anyway. If the event is Day 0, then Days 4, 3 and 2 should involve an increased level of carbohydrate intake (a 10-20% increase in carbohydrates as a proportion of your total calorie intake).

Proteins

The 15-25% of your diet made up of proteins is crucial for the repair, recovery and growth of your body and so is a very important part of a physically demanding challenge schedule.

Meat proteins:

Poultry and turkey (best eaten without the skin), lean cuts of beef/lamb/pork, fresh fish, rabbit.

"Everybody is different and it is crucial to take time to ascertain what brings out the best results in you. Some people cannot ingest high GI carbohydrates just before exercising and some people need a higher overall carbohydrate intake. The important thing is for each individual to test what works during their training. It can take you 4-6 weeks to figure out what works best and that could mean the difference between feeling good and feeling great."

Kathryn Bistany, Corpotential Limited

Non-meat proteins:

All plant products (except for soy) are low in one or more amino acids resulting in incomplete proteins if eaten on their own. However, when mixed with other foods, they can make complete proteins, so aim for a mixture of legumes (beans, peas, lentils) grains, nuts, seeds, vegetables and corn.

Fats and oils

Although 25-35% of your diet should be made up of fats, this should consist of good quality vegetable and animal fats. If you are struggling to find enough good fats within your diet, then foods such as humous, almonds and avocados are ideal. Oils from fish and nuts are a great source of energy and vital for the proper digestion of proteins. Other healthy oils include olive oil, flaxseed oil, rapeseed oil and omega oil. Omega-3 is found in cold water fish such as salmon, mackerel, herring and tuna as well as flaxseed and omega-6 in vegetable oils, nuts and seeds.

Avoid hydrogenated or trans fats (often found in baked goods and snacks) and eat saturated fats (found in butter, cheese, fatty meats and coconut and palm oils) in moderation.

Daily Nutritional Schedule

"The quality of the oils you choose is vital. All oils should be cold-pressed otherwise the heating process oxidises them and make them toxic to our system."

Kathryn Bistany, Corpotential Limited

- Aim to divide your daily nutritional intake into 6 smaller meals
- Kick start your day with a large low GI breakfast
- The balance of each meal should roughly reflect the balance of your whole diet: 50-60% carbs, 15-25% protein, 25-35% fats
- Try and leave 2-3 hours after eating and before going to bed

Eating whilst training/competing

- Leave 1-2 hours after eating a meal and before exercising
- After about 30 minutes of exercise start taking on calories: a person of average size and weight should aim to consume 50-100 calories every 30 minutes thereafter.
- During sessions of under 90 minutes all carbohydrate intake should be in liquid form.
- Find small, easily digestible high GI carbs that suit you for just before exercising and during long periods of exertion, e.g. energy bars/gels, dried fruit, bananas.
- Avoid doubling up: do not mix high energy foods with high energy drinks: either snack and water OR energy drink.

 Practise your fuelling routine thoroughly during your training. Come race day the last thing you want to do is experiment with different fuels to which you might be intolerant and which could seriously affect your performance.

Eating on a Challenge Expedition

On an ideal expedition there would be the time, the resources and the available food to fulfil a perfectly balanced daily diet. Unfortunately, this is rarely the case and when combined with the restrictions that a full programme of exercise puts on eating large meals, it can be very difficult to take on enough good food. It is vital, however, to make food one of your main priorities. If you start to lose weight and get run down on a long challenge expedition then a cycle of illness, injury and stunted progress will take over. Trying to get ahead in your schedule by cutting meal times short and saving money by skimping on the shopping budget is highly inadvisable. Time and money spent on eating is never wasted.

Your routine:

- Breakfast and lunch will represent about a quarter each of your calories for the day. Avoid heavy, rich or large meals, which will take time and energy to digest.
- Take on carbohydrate snacks during the day at regular intervals. Snack at the beginning of breaks and try and leave about 15 minutes before starting again.
- Lunch needs to give you a more sustained energy boost but avoid taking on copious, rich or heavy foods, which will use up energy to digest. A substantial lunch break is needed to allow food to settle.
- Plan the large meal of the day in the evening, when you have the necessary time to prepare, digest and enjoy it.

Food tips:

- Porridge or muesli are ideal breakfasts, best eaten with fruit.
- In cold conditions make up a flask of hot drink while you are eating.
- Good snacks are cereal/oatmeal bars, nuts, dried/fresh fruit, honey and peanut butter
- Eat chocolate in moderation and save some in your emergency rations
- If you are having a long lunch break you can eat low and medium GI carbohydrates, along with small portions of fish or chicken, for example.
- For shorter breaks, medium and high GI carbohydrates are preferable.
- The evening meal can be heavier and more filling, so take on plenty of rice, pasta or potatoes as well as lots of vegetables and some meat
- Carry herbs/spices and salt and pepper with you to add flavour to your cooking or local cuisine

- Dried, tinned and packaged food can often be low in vitamins and minerals, so carry some supplements to use if you feel your diet is deficient in a particular area.
- Practise cooking some stew dishes before you leave, as these are ideal for getting everything you need from one pot

Food hygiene is vital when you are cooking on an expedition, so don't cut corners and become careless about it. Clean all utensils thoroughly; wash and peel or boil vegetables and fruit; wash your hands with soap before you begin eating; store cooking and eating utensils in clean containers.

Eating Locally

Experiencing the tastes that your host country has to offer adds to your adventure and is an essential part of travelling. In many parts of the world you will find people particularly friendly and receptive to what you are doing, as well as very willing to share their food and offer you their hospitality. This is not to be missed. However, the daily physical exertion of a challenge expedition and a potentially tight schedule makes illness rather consequential. Freshly prepared hot food is normally a safe bet, but if you are particularly suspicious of something you are offered, then you may have to very politely decline.

Problem areas:

- Food left standing warm
- Rare meat, fish (especially shellfish)
- Unpeeled or uncooked fruit and vegetables; unwashed salads
- Raw or undercooked eggs
- Ice-cream
- Ice cubes made from tap water
- Unpasteurised dairy products

Weight Reduction

A challenge event can be an ideal focus for those wanting to lose weight. However, training without the necessary nutritional intake will significantly affect your progress and your health. If you plan to lose weight during your training for a challenge then you must do it sensibly and carefully.

- Eat small portions regularly – get into a routine of eating every 3½ to 4 hours
- Make sure there is plenty of variety and colour in your meals
- Carbohydrates are a vital part of a healthy diet and even more so if you are undertaking a full training programme, so do not miss them out – just make sure you eat the right ones
- Cut out saturated fats from your diet as much as possible
- Just because a product is "low fat" does not make it good for you – check out the levels of additives, preservatives, sugar and sweeteners
- Don't miss meals – in the short term this will make you crave high GI foods, in the longer term this will slow down your metabolism and encourage the body to more readily store fat reserves
- Cut out all high GI snacks
- Reduce your alcohol and caffeine intake
- DON'T try and lose weight leading up to a challenge event or during a challenge.

2. Fluids

When you exercise you get hotter, through increased blood flow and muscular work. The body's means of keeping you cool is to sweat, which is delivered from the blood to the surface of the skin. When exercising it is absolutely vital that this water is replaced. It is estimated that for every 1% drop in body weight due to dehydration there is a 5% drop in performance. A loss of 4% can cause exhaustion and if you continue to exercise while dehydrated you put your health in serious danger.

We lose, on average, between 500 and 1000ml of fluid for every hour of exercise. 1000ml is the equivalent of 1kg of body weight, so the effects of dehydration are very clear if you weigh yourself after training. Another good sign is the colour and quantity of your urine: pale and plentiful normally means that you are well hydrated, dark and sparse means that you are dehydrated.

Pale and plentiful urine after heavy exercise can mean that the water is not being absorbed due to lack of electrolytes, which can be found in sports drinks. After heavy exercise and particularly in hot conditions you will require electrolytes or at the very least some slow release sodium.

Fluid Intake

- Before exercise aim to drink 300-500ml of fluid 15 minutes prior to beginning the session
- During exercise aim to drink small amounts regularly - between 150-250ml every 15-20 minutes
- After exercise drink until your body weight (when naked) and urine are back to normal. This will probably be around 500ml, but you should aim to be drinking 1.5litres of fluid for every 1kg lost in body weight.

What Fluid?

Water is ideal for exercise that has not caused profuse sweating over a long period of time. For example, low/moderate exercise that lasts for under an hour in normal conditions should not normally result in salty sweating and therefore should not require extra sodium intake. However, everyone is different, so whatever exercise you do if your sweat is opaque, salty and leaving white marks on your clothes, or simply if you have sweated a lot for a sustained period, then you should try a sports drink containing sodium. Most sports drinks also contain 5-8% carbohydrate, which is what makes them 'isotonic' (of similar concentration to blood) and therefore quickly absorbed.

 Alcohol and exercise do not mix. Drinking alcohol before training clearly has a detrimental effect on co-ordination and performance. If you plan to have a drink after training or competing then make sure that you rehydrate with water or sports drinks fully beforehand. Remember that alcohol and caffeine are diuretics, causing dehydration.

Avoiding Injury

Following the above training principles and combining them with the nutritional principles in this chapter, will lay the foundations for healthy training. In addition to these I would advise getting a full health check from your doctor, particularly if you have decided to undertake a physical challenge that is in a different league to anything that you have attempted previously or if you have any medical problem or condition. There are essentially two types of sports injuries:

- Those caused by an acute 'traumatic' episode, such as tripping over
- Overuse' injuries, which are a result of repetitive overloading on a tissue.

"At the onset of injury – notice the word onset – stop what you are doing and rest. Nothing good is going to happen if you keep training with an injury. Our own rule of thumb is to take three days off. In many cases the inflammation that was causing pain will subside substantially in 3 days. If it doesn't, take 3 more off. If it still hurts, it's time to get professional help."

John Bingham and Jenny Hadfield, **Marathon Running for Mortals**

I would love to be able to give you a list of things to do to avoid injury. Unfortunately, this is not possible. The best advice is to listen to your body and follow all the training guidelines. On top of this, you can considerably reduce your likelihood of getting by incorporating the following into your training.

"The triad of health is a person's interaction within the environment. This includes mind, body and spirit. A dysfunction in any one of these areas will result in a compromise in overall health. A dysfunction in one area will affect another part. Homeostasis is a measure of all three systems working in unison."

James Gero: Sports Medicine and Performance Enterprises

Avoiding trauma injuries

- Choose and check equipment and clothing carefully
- Train in a well lit environment and ensure you are visible when outdoors
- Do not train when your alertness is compromised, through tiredness or substances for example

Avoiding overuse injuries

- Increase your workload gradually – never crash train
- Include sufficient rest and recovery in your schedule
- Get medical advice for prolonged soreness, pain or discomfort
- Warm up and warm down
- Include core stability and flexibility work in your sessions
- Avoid muscle imbalance by following a balanced resistance programme
- Spend time on your technique and get expert advice if possible
- Use appropriate equipment and clothing

- Take account of environmental conditions, such as extreme heat or cold
- Stay hydrated and eat well.

Reducing Your Chances of Injury

Apart from training safely and sensibly (and seeking medical advice if you have any concerns about your physical condirion) here are the three most important ways of minimising your risk of injury.

1. Diet

What you eat is crucual to your body's ability to fight illness and avoid and recover from injury. Look at pages 162 to 168 carefully.

Certain foods will inhibit repair whilst others will promote it.

If injured, be it a minor sprain or a more serious break, try and comply with the following:

- Avoid all refined sugar, sweets, biscuits, chocolates etc.
- Avoid saturated fats in fatty meats and dairy products
- Avoid all junk and processed foods
- Increase intake of legumes, fruits and vegetables
- Increase protein intake in the form of lean meats, chicken (without the skin) and fish
- Increase omega-3 intake

Kathryn Bistany, Corpotential Limited

2. Flexibility

Flexibility helps improve performance and also reduces the likelihood of injury, and along with core stability exercises, should be something that everyone should encompass in their training sessions. When it comes to the challenge itself, particularly if its demands are prolonged, good flexibility will considerably reduce the

project ought to include in their schedule. Good core stability will improve your form, stability, control, power and help reduce the likelihood of injury. For a full programme ask for some advice from a qualified trainer or physiotherapist.

"Tried and tested for over 5000 years, yoga offers series of techniques ranging from the physical -breath control and postures, to mind control -meditation, hand gestures and chanting, all of which can greatly improve your flexibility and work on core strength and stamina."

Yogi Dr Malik, Editor of YOGA magazine

soreness and aches and pains that are associated with exercising for long periods on consecutive days. For a flexibility programme that suits your needs consult a qualified trainer or physiotherapist.

3. Core Stability

Apart from strength work that is specifically related to your challenge, this is an area of resistance training that everyone undertaking an endurance

It is impossible to move one part of the body without affecting the mechanics of another regardless of how distant they are, therefore whilst training bare this in mind. An example of this: An athlete with poor running mechanics may induce an excessive lower limb rotation with a counter rotation of the femur causing possibly a pelvic dysfunction and consequently lower back pain. This in term creates a functional scoliosis which plays stress on the local musculature and pain further up the back. The cycle continues. He goes to seek help for his back. However the back will never really heal until the foot and running mechanics are solved. Therefore it is wise to become observant and in this case the athlete may have noticed his shoes were heavily warn on either edge showing signs of excessive pronation or supination

James Gero: Sports Medicine and Performance Enterprises

Long-haul challenge expeditions represent a huge physical and mental test of endurance, so make sure that you get enough rest. Here, Chris Field and Willl Lenton down their tools and make their own shade before continuing on unsupported towards Alaska from Argentina, raising £18,000 for Médecins San Frontières.

If you plan to add an interesting angle to your challenge then make sure you fully understand the physical implications and train accordingly. Brothers, Steve and Pete Fleming kicked a football 250 miles across Malawi. They sought the advice of Craig Sharp, Professor of Sports Science, Brunel University: "Kicking a ball over 250 miles in ten days is a formidable challenge. It means covering a marathon distance every day for ten days, at an uneven gait due to the need for kicking the ball. If each kick is roughly ten metres, to keep the ball under reasonable control, then over approximately 400,000 metres that imples 40,000 kicks."

Challenge Profile:

Kyrgyzstan to Pakistan for Scotland's Alternative Skiiers

Karen Darke

Born 1971 – Learning Development Consultant

The Challenge - Kyrgyzstan to Pakistan by Bicycle & Handcycle

The route from Kyrgyzstan to Pakistan took us through the Tien Shan Mountains, Pamirs, Karakoram, finishing along the Karakoram Highway. We decided on this because of the desire of the team to visit this region and to journey through a range of different cultures and scenery, but primarily as an obvious, quiet(ish) road through the mountains that would be navigable by handcycle.

This was my first major expedition since breaking my back in a climbing accident and becoming paralysed so it was a huge personal challenge.

The team was made up of four people - one tandem handbike and two mountain bikes. One MTB had a trailer to tow the wheelchair. It took us six months to complete the challenge.

The Charity - Scotland's Alternative Skiiers

The SAS Club was founded in October 1989 out of the necessity to help provide skiing facilities, equipment and opportunities for disabled people in Scotland. At present only a small percentage of disabled people can experience the thrills and exhilaration which the sport of skiing can offer.

This is a charity which helped me to access the mountains again after my accident.

We raised a total of £10,000 for the charity. It was also very important for me to raise awareness of disability and inclusion in the UK. By undertaking a successful expedition with an inclusive team that attracted some positive media attention, we were able to raise the profile of what disabled explorers can achieve (see pages 19 & 20 for more information). Hopefully we inspired and motivated others to achieve their goals and dreams, and shared information with other disabled people on how to take on their own inclusive challenge.

Fundraising Tip
Set up a Justgiving web-page, change the page regularly and use it as a point of contact for everyone from friends to journalists. Give regular e-mail up-dates of progress.

Diary

Best Moment

Reaching the top of the Khunjerab Pass (China – Pakistan border) and then cycling downhill for a week through the Karakoram mountains! The unbelieveable sense of being in mountains again, and the relief and freedom of that feeling.

"This was a life-changing trip for me personally – my first major expedition after becoming paralysed, which helped me to realize what was possible, push my boundaries, and access an environment which is important to me - the mountains - in a manner which really, I believe, allows the environment to be explored and felt. There is no glass barrier between you and the world!"

Hardest Moment

Running out of food and one of the MTBs breaking down (crank) within 20km of the expedition's highest point (top of Khunjerab Pass).

Biggest Problem

We had some mechanical problems and when things went wrong we didn't always have the skills to fix them. The broken crank on the bicycle was a good example, particularly as we didn't have a crank tool!

Training Tip
Motivation! Get out there and do it, come rain or shine. Every bit counts!

We would have had huge problems crossing the Kyrgyz – China border if we had not had the correct advance paperwork and visas in place. We met others who had been turned back because they had not organized anything in advance.

Karen Darke and her tandem partner make their way through the Tiien Shan Mountains towards Pakistan

173

Running

Runner's World are leaders in this field and provide hundreds of thousands of runners with expert advice through some of the best magazine and printed resources available. Check out More Information (page 175) for details of where to look.

Running is the most popular way of taking on a challenge for charity and there are events out there of every shape and size, from a 5km fun run to the Sri Chinmoy 3100 mile running race, the longest foot race in the world. You will clearly need to pitch your training at the right level, so having read the following tips for all challenges, take a look at some of the resources available for your needs and experience.

3 Tips for All Runners

- Running is high impact and most runners will experience overuse injuries at some point, so increase your activity levels very gradually, and avoid increasing mileage by more than 10% every week.

- Technique is particularly important for runners. With every imprecise pound of the foot, you could be doing yourself damage. Expert advice on your running style and appropriate trainers are invaluable.

- Try and find a training partner of similar ability. Your charity may be able to put you in touch with someone in your area running for them in the same event, or you could join a running club.

Beginners "Few people can run a full mile the first time out the door, so don't even try. You'll get discouraged and quit. Instead, mix running and walking. Run for 30 seconds, walk for 90 seconds, and repeat this nine more times for a total of 20 minutes four times a week with this 30/90 – second pattern, change your run/walk ratio to 75/45 and repeat the four times a week pattern. Next comes 60/60, then 75/45, then 90/30. Eventually, you'll be running for several minutes at a time between walking breaks, and then – hallelujah! – you'll be able to run for 20 minutes without stopping."
Runners World

Form and Technique

- Head – Erect, eyes looking forward to a point on the ground about 20 metres away.
- Shoulders and arms – Keep shoulders level and square, with arms swinging freely and comfortable back and forth; elbows bent at around 90°.
- Hands – A relaxed fist, with the thumb resting lightly on the forefinger
- Torso – Erect with the chest up, without slumping or leaning forwards or back
- Hips – Square and level
- Legs – A relaxed action with perpendicular movements
- Feet – Pointing straight ahead and landing directly under the hips

Running Shoes

As a runner this is by far your most important purchase and one that I would very strongly advise you to spend time and money on. You need to find running shoes that suit your running style and your foot type and this will make running more comfortable and injury free.

Pronation

Pronation describes what happens to your foot when it hits the ground and rolls from heel to toe.

- A neutral pronator hits the outside of the heel and rolls evenly up to the ball of the foot, which distributes the stress consistently across the foot.
- Underpronation is when there is not enough roll from the edge of the heel to the ball, so the outside of the foot takes too much stress
- Overpronation involves too much roll from outside to inside. This often causes lower leg and knee injuries.

Which one am I?
- Look at your shoes – If they are particularly worn on the inside (medial) then you overpronate, on the outside (lateral) then you underpronate and if they are worn uniformly across the foot then you are neutral
- Go to a running centre/specialist shop – These great places have experts on hand to look at your running style, often on a running machine, and give you guidance.

Shopping for Trainers

- Go to a specialist running shop with your old trainers/shoes and give them information about your challenge, your weight, your experience and your target weekly mileage.
- Wear the socks you will wear when you run
- Avoid buying latest fad trainers or ones that offer an ingenious gimmick
- If you plan to wear orthotics take them with you

Fit Checks

- Press your thumb into the shoe just beyond your big toe – there should be a thumb width from the top of the shoe to the top of your toe.
- At the widest part of your foot the shoe should not be too tight or allow room for your foot to slide around
- Your heel should not slide up and down as you walk or run
- Try and feel the trainers in action – some shops have running machines

Additional tip
If you are running in intense heat, your feet are most likely to swell. This is often as much as a shoe size larger. It is advisable therefore to buy a larger size for the purpose of the challenge, not forgetting to put some miles into the shoes before hand, and adding an insole that can consequently be removed. If running an ultra and you have a support crew then often taking two of three types of shoes can be like getting a massage on your feet during the race, however you need to experiment with this in training as it does not suit everybody

More Information for Runners
Runners' World magazine is available monthly and at **www.runnersworld. co.uk** you can access a massive range of resources, includng a great search facility for finding the right charity for you.

The Marathon Guide

A marathon is an awesome challenge. 26.2 miles of sweat. If you take one on you will never forget the elation of crossing the finish line and the satisfaction of always knowing that you could do it.

Training Tips

- Aim to increase the distance you run by no more than 10% each week
- Your maximum training distance should be between 15 and 20 miles, or the equivalent of 90 to 120 minutes exercise – this approximately represents your body's glycogen storage limit
- Make sure that you include long runs every other week, which should be about 150% of that week's normal distance
- Although you have to keep your weekly mileage up, include some cross training in your schedule

Leading up to the event

- Your final long run, which should be done 10-14 days before the event, should more or less dictate the pace at which you aim to run the race
- Taper your training as you approach the marathon. Some coaches advise reducing your training by as much as 50% during the last two to three weeks before the event, as well as almost no running in the final 2/3 days. This allows damaged muscle fibres to heal and promotes maximum glycogen storage.
- Increase your carbohydrate intake during the 4-5 days preceding the day before the marathon

The Day Before

- Keep water with you at all times and stay hydrated
- By this stage you should have completed most of your carbo-loading, so don't over eat – regular and small balanced meals
- Avoid being on your feet all day
- Make a priority of getting a good night's sleep
- Lay out everything you need for the following day and decide upon the morning's schedule

Race day

- Get up early enough to have a small and light breakfast to be finished about 2 hours before the race
- Consider eating a light snack, such as a cereal bar or banana, about 30 minutes before the race
- Aim to drink around 500ml of water or sports drink about 10-20 minutes before the race
- Go through your usual warm up and stretching routine. Don't try anything different, even if everyone around you is
- Get to the start line early – you don't want to feel panicky
- Be confident in your preparation… there is nothing left to do but run.

The Race

- Do not let the adrenaline make you fly out of the blocks – find the pace that you established in the final long runs and stick to it as closely as possible, checking your watch at mile markers for guidance. A good way is to write mile times for the first 5 miles on the back of your hand and then miles 10, 13, 18, 21, 26 or something like this
- Do not pass by the fluid stations and

- aim to drink 150-250 ml of water or sports drink every 15-20 minutes
- Consider switching from water to sports drinks after about 60 minutes
- Snack as you felt comfortable doing in training – fruit, sports bars/gels and

"The ability to cope with race day nerves is vital if you want to fulfil your potential and can mean the difference between an under-par or a personal best performance."

Jason Henderson, Athletics Weekly

cereal bars all provide a quick source of carbohydrate during the race.

After the Race

- Keep walking if possible and don't lie down, however tempting
- Rehydrate fully, aiming to drink 500-1000ml of water/sports drink
- Eat whatever you crave and take on a balance of carbs, protein and

minerals to replenish energy stores, enhance muscle repair and replace lost minerals.
- Get medical attention as soon as possible if you need it
- Warm down within 20 minutes of finishing
- Get a post race massage if you can
- Avoid long, hot soaks in the bath, as it may aggravate muscle soreness and cause swelling. Although it may not be what you really want, soaking your legs in cold water will reduce inflammation

"Preparing for a marathon is no easy thing. It is a big, big time commitment, and for most it demands vast amounts of energy -- physical, mental and emotional. The pay-off, of course, is equally enormous. Enhanced strength, confidence and stoicism are the treasures reaped by all marathon athletes, whatever their ability."

Josh Clarke, www.coolrunning.com

Some of the 30,000 runners in the London Marathon in 2003

Cycling

Accompanying you in this section are experts from **CTC**, the UK's national cyclists' organisation. The CTC can provide you with resources and advice to help you take on your cycling challenge successfully.

Anybody, of any age and fitness, can achieve something remarkable and hugely rewarding on a bike. Whether it is a 20km ride or a 6 month epic, preparing for a cycling challenge is about a combination of gradually conditioning yourself to the exercise and understanding how to get the most out of your bike. And most importantly it is about enjoying yourself.

3 Top cycling tips

- Make cycling a part of your everyday routine, using your bike to commute, go to the shops or for any daily route that you might normally cover by car, bus or train.
- Cycling is a great way to see the countryside and spend time with your family and friends, so take day trips as often as you can. By making cycling a fun and sociable part of your life you will be far less intimidated by the challenge ahead.
- Be specific in your preparation and make sure that you are training for your particular challenge.
  - If your challenge involves a lot of climbing then include plenty of hill sessions in training.
  - If your bike is going to weigh 50kg in total, then train with gradually more weight attached to it until you are comfortable with this amount.
  - If you are planning to cycle a number of consecutively long days, then practise doing this - consider planning a few long weekends of cycling in preparation.
  - If you have a target time, or have to cover certain distances, then train to gradually become comfortable with this pace.

Safety Tips

- Be Aware - As a cyclist you must be constantly aware of other vehicles, the quality of the road and your own position on it
- Be Seen - Buy and maintain front and rear lights for your bike and wear high visibility clothing
- Check your equipment - Make sure that:
  - the saddle and handlebars are adjusted to the right height
  - the gears and brakes in good working order
  - your helmet fits snugly
  - the chain is well lubricated
  - the tyres are in good condition and are inflated to the correct pressure
  - your lights work and have sufficient power for your journey
- Remain within the law - check the Highway code and consider taking a training course

Many people think cycling is a lot more dangerous than it actually is. Health experts estimate that the exercise benefits outweigh any risks by 20:1.
Kevin Mayne, CTC

Top CTC Tips for Equipment

Get a bike that fits you

A bike is a super efficient conversion of human energy in to forward motion. But it only works well if your muscles work well, and some time spent setting up your bike can work wonders. If you are not sure what to do phone your local CTC group who will recommend a suitable shop, or invite you along to get set up on one of their rides. If you are buying a new bike CTC has information on types of bikes.

Buy the right equipment

Concentrate on those parts of the body that contact the bike for maximum comfort; and most important of all, the tender parts in contact with the bike seat. Cycling shorts are designed as a one-piece garment with an absorbent liner that is worn without underwear. A couple of pairs mean you can keep them spotlessly clean, and there are different designs for men and women.

After shorts the other priority will be shoes. Training shoes are designed to flex when running, cycling shoes are stiff, to transfer energy to the pedals.

Reduce drag

On a road cycling challenge, if you have a mountain bike, ask your local shop to replace the knobbly tyres with road tyres. On all bikes keep the tyres pumped to the manufacturers' recommended pressure. This will make the ride more comfortable, reduce puncture risk and most importantly, make the ride easier. (Don't forget a pump, tyre levers and a spare inner tube).

Top CTC Tip for Technique

Pedal – don't push

When experienced cyclists and new users mix, the most obvious difference to an outside observer is usually pedalling speed. The comfortable mile-eating rhythm that enables even unfit riders to cover long distances comes through practice, but the most notable feature is higher pedalling rates in lower gears. Over-gearing is like subjecting yourself to a weight training session that goes on for hours, and your stiff legs after the ride will confirm it.

Practise pedalling slightly faster than feels comfortable normally, and as you get used to it up the tempo again. When you ride with a CTC group try to pedal at the same rate as others by selecting different gears. A range of 85-100 pedal revolutions per minute is normal for a smooth cyclist.

More Information

For more information on all of these topics go to **www.ctc.org.uk** and take advantage of a wide range of excellent resources. CTC operates the National Cycle Training Helpline and can find a qualified instructor anywhere in the UK.

CTC members get discounts at their mail order shop and on cycle and recovery insurance which is the equivalent to the motorist's "get you home" cover.

Walking & Hiking

The Ramblers' Association is Britain's biggest walking charity that has been working for 70 years to promote walking and to improve conditions for everyone who walks in England, Scotland and Wales.

You can go pretty much anywhere on your own two feet, no matter your age or fitness. Walking challenges can be set at any level, making them accessible for those of all ages and abilities. For more details on walking in the UK and on the needs of your specific challenge, look at More Information.

3 Top Walking & Hiking Tips

- Make walking an important part of your daily routine –
  - Try and change your commute to include 20-30 minutes of walking
  - Take the stairs whenever possible
  - Walk for 30 minutes during your lunch break
- Find a hiking/walking route, comparable in terrain to your challenge route, that you will be able to complete 2-4 times a month. This will act as your pacing walk/hike through which your progress can be measured.
- For self-sufficient challenges, gradually increase the weight in your pack until you are comfortable carrying it for a period at least as long as your event or daily distance will require.
  - If you are a beginner or out of touch, then begin with a daypack of 5-7kg and 10% more (i.e. 0.5-0.7kg in this instance) each session/week until you reach your target pack weight.
  - To simulate the weight of camping equipment and clothes during training avoid using rocks or large weights. Heavy ropes, clothes, water bottles and if necessary small weights are more suitable.

If your challenge involves hiking through remote areas and in harsh conditions, or if it encompasses mountaineering, then aquiring the necessary skills and experience is essential. Look through the reference section for more resources in this area.

Ramblers' Tips for Technique

- Start by assuming a straight posture, with spine and neck straight, chin parallel to the ground and eyes level, shoulders relaxed, arms hanging loose, belly pulled in and pelvis tucked under slightly.
- Allow your arms to swing in time to your stride with elbows bent and hands cupped. Try to keep your eyes ahead for most of the time.
- Breathe deeply, expanding your stomach, and try to breathe in rhythm with your steps.
- If you're carrying a backpack, adjust the straps and use the hip belt if provided to ensure it's carried high on the back.

Importance of Footwear

Appropriate footwear for hiking challenges is made to withstand tough conditions and the additional weight of a backpack, as well as offer extensive support for your feet and ankles.

- Buy your boots/shoes at least a month, and preferably 3-4 months, before you set off and wear them as often as you can.
- Know exactly what you want the boot to do: terrain, weather, vegetation distance, pack weight etc.
- Test the boot as thoroughly as the supplier/outlet will allow
- The fit should be snug and comfortable, with no sliding, pinching, tightness, rubbing or chaffing
- Your heel should not lift up away from the sole and you should be able to wiggle your toes

Ramblers' Tips for Mountain Walking Equipment

- Essentials - Warm and waterproof clothing, a map, compass and good navigation skills
- Advisable
- A survival bag: a heavy-duty bag for body insulation in an emergency
  - A torch and spare batteries
  - A whistle
  - Additional warm clothing, including hat and gloves
  - High-energy rations such as mint cake, chocolate, dried fruit
  - Water purification tablets
  - A first-aid kit

Ramblers' General Safety Tips

- Don't take unnecessary risks by tackling overly long or difficult routes.
- Know where you are or have a map and the ability to read it.
- On longer walks, be aware of "escape routes" in case you need to cut your walk short for whatever reason.
- Make sure you have plenty to eat and drink and are adequately dressed for the length of time you'll be out.
- Take a sensible approach to the weather, which in Britain is rarely severe but changeable and often wet. Check the forecast before you set out (try the Met Office), always take a waterproof and keep an eye on the sky. Rain, mist or fog and cold are the obvious hazards, but strong winds can be a problem especially on exposed hillsides or coastal cliffs.
- Make sure someone knows when you expect to be back.

More Information

For information on every imaginable aspect of walking and hiking go to www.ramblers.org.uk, phone 020 7339 8500 or e-mail their experts at ramblers@london.ramblers.org.uk

Recording and Monitoring

How to record and monitor your conditioning is left till the very end of the physical challenge because it affects every aspect of your preparation. Record everything, monitor everything.

When you are preparing your training schedule, with the help of the planning principles on page 156 and 157, and with a personal trainer or gym instructor, design it to allow room for recording the results of each sessions, assessing your physical condition and evaluating your overall progress. Knowing exactly where you are and where you have been will inform the next stage of planning and will improve your confidence in your progress.

Also keep notes on your equipment, your diet and any illness or injuries that you experience.

Day	Session	Time/Distance	Notes
Mon	Run 30 mins, 70% HR	6km	Morning, rain. Felt tired, disappointed with 6km
Tues	Intervals: 6x75 secs @ max 85% HR, rest 3 min walk	Max 350m, min 300	Lunch break, fine. Sore after Mon, need to warm down for longer. Legs not fresh
Wed	Circuit Training 40 mins 4xcircuit of 6 exercises	1. 15x50kg 2. 15x30kg 3.15x25kg 4. 50 reps 5. 60 reps 6. 20 reps	Morning, cold. Felt good, much better than last week. Legs felt fresh after long warm down on Tues and long warm up at start.
Thur	REST		Woke up with sore legs, but eased during the day
Fri	Intervals: 6x60 secs @ 75% effort, rest 3 min	Max 300m, min 240m	fter work, cold & windy. Improved recovery quite quickly – can shorten to 150secs walk
Sat	Run 40 mins, 60% HR	8km	Morning, fine. Felt restricted by HR. Can lengthen longer run
Sun	Rest - Active Recovery	30 mins light swim	Eased sore legs considerably

Organisation

Fundraising is hard work and frustrating, but ultimately very rewarding. Physical conditioning is tough and requires endless reserves of willpower, but will make you look and feel healthier. Logistical and administrative organisation is time-consuming and pretty dull, but...well...in fact it doesn't really have that much of an upside.

However, your challenge, whether its planning is in your hands or in those of a charity, event organiser or operator, must be well planned. This section will help you make the process efficient and effective.

The First Steps for All Charity Challenges

1. Aims

Produce a document that lays out the overarching aims of your project.

Write down what you want to do and why. This may be simply a personal document or one that forms the basis of a proposal. Be completely honest and remember that there is neither a right reason nor a "good" justification for taking on a charity challenge. That you want to lose weight and look heroic is just as valid at this stage as contributing to a cause that you feel strongly about. Your document should include:

- A single statement of no more than 100 words
- A number of supporting objectives that cover every aspect of the project as they are conceived
- A fundraising target

2. Timeline

Write a timeline of the project and its organisation.

You need to include target dates for the challenge, training, fundraising and every aspect of organisation. Here are some examples of the deadlines that you might face:

- Deadlines for grant applications can sometimes come only once a year, or demand a period of up to nine months before the project takes place. See some of the grant-giving bodies listed on the website for more details.

- If individual participants in a team or group challenge are being asked to cover their own costs they need to be given enough time to raise the necessary funds.

- Up to six months is needed to plan large fundraising events and remember that diaries and schedules fill up very early for weekends and holiday periods, just as venues and services need booking in advance.
- You need to plan about six months

in advance to find a suitable date and apply for street collection permissions. See page 93 for more details

- Flights/trains/coaches booked a long way in advance represent considerable savings

- Vaccinations for foreign travel need to take place at least four months before travelling. See page 197 for more details.

- Liquor Licences needed to raise money from the sale of alcohol usually take a minimum of 3 months to obtain. See page 93 for more details.

- If you plan to take a vehicle abroad, the permissions and insurance needs can be very time-consuming. See page 197 for more details.

- VISAS sometimes need to be applied for up to three months before departure. If you plan to involve voluntary work then the process can be longer. See page 197 for more details.

- Lengthy and unpredictable decision-making processes within companies for sponsorship requests.

- A turnaround of rarely less than two weeks and often up to three months for individuals to respond to sponsorship letters

3. Budget

Draw up an estimated budget for the project

Whether you plan to run a marathon or take on a year-long trek, write down all the projected costs as realistically as possible.

During the fundraising process which you may or may not have started, you must establish what you need. In drawing up a budget you are expanding upon this list and making a more accurate estimation of their cost.

Divide these budet items into three areas:

1. Relatively normal expenditure that you are willing to absorb (e.g. printing, postage, gym membership etc.)

2. Exceptional expenditure that you are able to cover (e.g. specialist equipment)

3. Exceptional expenditure that you are not willing or able to cover (e.g. flights, accomodation)

See more advice on expeditions finance and budgeting on pages 204-205.

Challenge Profile

Calcutta to London for Future Hope

Chris Proctor

Born 1980 – Film-maker

The Challenge - Calcutta to London by Classic Motorbike

I had been working as a Development Officer for Future Hope in Calcutta and was due to come home to England. However, I felt it would be more interesting to head back overland which in turn appeared to be a good way of raising some funds for Future Hope and awareness for the plight of street and working children.

The route went through Nepal, India, Kazakhstan, Russia, Belarus, Poland, Germany, Holland and England. Being on a motorbike leaves you more exposed and accessible to the people you meet along the way, allowing you to head where other forms of transport won't allow.

The very nature of the adventure seemed to draw people in, be it sponsors, patrons, pledges, or media coverage. It was nice to be able to strike a balance between good old fashioned adventure and raising the profile of these children.

The Charity - Future Hope

Future Hope India was set up to provide a home, education, medical aid and opportunity to some of the street children of Kolkata (Calcutta). Many of these children suffer extreme poverty and have little or no ability to change their lives. Future Hope now runs five homes and a school for over 150 children.

Having worked as a Development officer within Future Hope I was familiar with the lives of street children in Calcutta. Seeing their determination, courage, optimism, and self belief gave me the confidence to believe that anything was possible. Knowing that this was the end of my time at the charity I felt I wanted to do something that would contribute in a different capacity both financially and by raising awareness of the issues throughout Asia and closer to home in Europe.

I raised over £45,000 for Future Hope and through media coverage and presentations was able to raise their profile in the UK.

Fundraising Tip
Total self belief, a willingness to make sacrifices, commitment to your goal and blind optimism - even when things seem to be in a state of chaos!

Diary

"This is an experience that will provide me with moments and relationships that I will cherish for the rest of my life."

Best Moment

It's hard to say, there were so many: finally leaving Calcutta after months of stress; crossing the Himalayas into Nepal; the vastness and isolation of Kazakhstan and Russia; vodka in yurt tents; freedom of the open road; friendships made; getting lost in England on the way to London and finally meeting friends and family at Buckingham Palace – shame the Queen couldn't make it though...

Hardest Moment

Having my inner tube blow on the first day out of Calcutta while crossing the most lawless state of India (Bihar). I was left stranded on the side of the road, at night with memories of stories of hijackings as my only companion.

Training Tip

Make sure you have envisaged every possibility. Assume the worst, as things always seem to go wrong. You have to feel confident that you can handle every situation.

Beyond this there were 14 hour stints in the saddle, sleep deprivation, drunken gun wielding boarder guards, breaking down in the Ural mountains, dodgy truck drivers, mutinous co riders, the list goes on...

Biggest Problem

To be honest the hardest part was keeping the team together. My Indian colleague had never left the country, was incredibly homesick and scared at times and often threatened to fly home due to the concern he would miss his wedding. Other than that, ensuring that you made it across the boarders despite not having the correct papers and getting your passport back from boarder guards, determined to take a bribe.

Chris and his team mate and camera operator, Molly Oldfield, on the road to Astana, Kazakhstan.

Organised Challenges

There is a hugely competitive market for organised challenges, from mass participation fun runs to overseas treks. Once you have decided that either an established event or a packaged challenge is for you, look carefully at the options and find organisers and operators that do things well.

Single-Day Events

Mass participation challenge events must conform to very strict legal guidelines to ensure the safety of participants, but they can be organised with vastly different degrees of professionalism. There are so many single-day events for each discipline and level of endurance that you can afford to shop around. Consider the following:

- Cost of registration and what you get in return (support, facilities etc.)
- How available are the places? Places in some major events can only be obtained through charities.
- Level of health and safety support at the event (fluid stations, medics etc)
- Access – What is done to ensure that everyone can get to the event?
- Facilities – Can you change at the event? What refreshments are available? What is there for spectators?
- Administration – What do they do to prevent large registration queues? What do you have to do on the day?
- Extras – Medical and equipment checkpoints, information and advice stations, massage areas, 'try and buy' stalls, discounts, family areas etc.
- Reputation of the event – Talk to someone that has participated and find out if they had any problems.

How to get a 'Golden Bond' Place

Golden Bonds are distributed by major events, most notably the London Marathon, to charities, which gives them a guaranteed number of places in the event. Each place is then distributed by the charities at their discretion. Follow these steps to give yourself the best chance of getting a secured place through a charity:

- Apply early for a place in the event through the ballot system
- Let your chosen charity/ies know that you have applied through the ballot system, but that if unsuccessful you would like to be considered for a Golden Bond place
- A charity distributing places wants to know that you will raise at least the minimum sponsorship and that you will collect and send in that money on time. The following will help reassure them of this:
  - Evidence of fundraising success
  - A brief breakdown your main intended areas of fundraising
  - How you will ensure money collection
  - That you are organised, competent and determined
  - A realistic ambition to raise more than the minimum target

Expeditions

The number of organised treks or cycles grows every year, as do the number of people who have wonderful experiences through participating in them. Similarly, every year charities and adventure travel operators are becoming increasingly aware of the need to plan challenges which are environmentally and ethically sensitive, with the cause as the focal point rather than simply the funds.

However, this does not mean that there is a universal standard of practice. It is sensible to try and match what you want to achieve and how, with the policies and practice of the charities and operators.

The Choices Section (More info on pages 25-56) will have given you an idea as to the cause and means of your organised adventure. From this point there are two choices.

- To register with your charity of choice on one of their overseas challenges

A team of Cancer Research UK Trek Peru participants

- To register with an independent, third party charity challenge operator and participate in the name of a particular charity

For either of these decisions you should try and take into consideration some of the following:

Participants

If you are going to be on the expedition with a group of total strangers, which can be immensely rewarding, then it is worth finding out how they have been assembled. Will you all be travelling at the same pace or divided up into different ability groups? How big is the expedition group?

Reputation & Experience

Find out as much as you can about the operator who is organising the challenge. They will undoubtedly have a long list of positive quotes from participants, but what has gone wrong on previous trips? Have they run this trip before? What qualifications and experience do the guides have? What local operators are they linked to and what is their experience and reputation like? Do they know the area and the route well, or do they specialise in a particular area?

"The relationship between the charity and their tour operator is a really good sign of how well previous trips have gone, so look out for strong and long standing partnerships."

Nicola Hanna, Shelter

191

Responsible Tourism

Overseas charity expeditions should be examples of absolute best practice. But is your operator or charity doing everything they can to tour responsibly?

Here are three important areas:

Small group sizes — Large groups of people travelling through relatively remote parts of the world with limited infrastructure will inevitably lead to greater impact on the natural environment and local peoples.

Employment of local staff & use of local facilities — Employing local staff and using local facilities heps sustain local communities (accommodation, restaurants etc) provides employment and supports the local economy.

Donation to overseas communities — Help the local communities as well as your chosen charity. Some tour operators also make donations per participant or per group to projects in the local communities where their expeditions take place, which is sometimes turned into a long-term commitment to development funding.

Victoria Bolton, Operations Manager, Charity Challenge

Health and Safety

Going into a foreign environment and undertaking a tough physical challenge in extreme conditions presents a number of obvious risks. What is being done to ensure that all the participants are prepared for these conditions? Will you be acclimatised to the altitude, heat or cold gradually? (More info on page 198) What contingency plans are in place? What medical support will be travelling with you? Have they visited the area and done a thorough risk assessment? Do you need to get your own insurance?

Cost effectiveness

You are totally within your rights to ask for a breakdown of how your money will be spent and how efficiently it will be used. Bear in mind that the administrative costs for charities and operators are high on such trips as you need a high level of support over a long period of time.

Support & Resources

What can the operator offer you in terms of fundraising and training resources and support? Bear in mind that although literature is very useful, it helps to be able to ring someone when questions or problems arise. Are there training sessions or weekends organised?

Offers & Discounts

Good operators can organise discounts for participants for every aspect of the expedition: gym membership, training and specialist clothing, equipment, flights etc.

Independent Challenges

If you plan to organise a challenge of your own then there are a lot of exciting decisions to be made. However, for the success of the project and the reputation of your charity, independent challenges have to be organised impeccably. This section will give you the organisational essentials for such challenges.

Even if you plan to sign up to a packaged challenge then it's important to understand what is involved in it's organisation nevertheless. Awareness of the necessary organisational tools, logistical procedures and administrative requirements will be very useful. Just because you will not be taking the decisions, does not mean that you will not have an important part to play.

1. Planning the Expedition

The Challenge Participants

If you plan to undertake an independently organised challenge as a team, then the choice of its members or the decision to join a particular group is crucial. Throughout the project you will be relying upon the motivation, the emotional stability, the honesty, the physical condition, the common sense, the skill, the ingenuity and the friendship of your team mates. With them you will be undergoing intense physical and emotional stress, that you may never have experienced before.

Similarly, you will be sharing a potentially life-changing and certainly unforgettable experience with your team. You may have to ask them to put their safety in your hands and yours in theirs. The trust and interdependence that can develop is a wonderful legacy of your challenge.

Your first decision may be whether to take on the challenge single-handedly or as part of a team.

1. Solo Challenges

Every aspect of the project, from the daily highs to the lows and from the organisational pressure to the final rush of achievement, will be magnified if you take it on alone. You must therefore be confident in your own ability and your own motivational skills. Frequently, you will come up against obstacles that you have to deal with alone. At the same time, success in coping with each of these obstacles and completing the challenge will ultimately be more extraordinary accomplishment. In reality and in the perception of potential supporters, the test of endurance is more substantial, making the solo challenge more inspirational. As your job is to inspire people to support you and your cause, this can be an important asset.

In 2000, journalist and writer Alexandra Pratt undertook a trip by canoe across the interior of Labrador and Quebec, aiming to trace the voyage of Mina Hubbard, an explorer who had been the first and only person to complete the journey 100 years previously. As a young woman arriving alone in Labrador with such a remarkable plan, Alex received enormous support and kindness from its citizens. The lifelong relationships that she developed were, in her opinion, a result of her decision to take the project on as a solo expeditioner. However, Labrador and the violent current of the river, were extremely testing for Alex and her guide. They could not complete the route and she had to pay a price for taking on the voyage with minimal resources and her determination to go it alone, and could cover only 100 of the 576 mile journey. This is very representative of the potential balance of advantages and disadvantages that going solo holds.

Tips for Solo Challengers
- Make a big deal of being solo and unsupported (if you are!) and use it to help you inspire support.
- Demonstrate total financial transparency, impeccable organisation and thorough contingency and safety planning.
- Ask for help - do not hesitate to be up front about the degree to which you need the support of others.
- Accumulate volunteers and supporters and delegate to people that you trust.

2. Group Challenges

With each new member come new ideas, new skills, new contacts, new sponsors and more support and enthusiasm. At every stage of the project, from the first line drawn on a map to the final hug of celebration, having a team of people, however big or small, to share everything, can add a tremendous amount. Good, reliable and committed team members represent halving of responsibility and doubling of capacity.

However, if the wrong people get involved for the wrong reasons, then the antagonism within the group can be destructive.

Putting a group together
Do not let the excitement of the idea distract the prospective members from understanding the nature of the commitment. If a few of you have come up with an idea together and you are all set on being a part of it, then talk very honestly about:
- what attracted you to the idea?
- what you want to achieve by it?
- how much time are you going to be able to commit to the whole project?

If you are an individual or a very small group there is a temptation to approach your best friends. There are obvious benefits to this, but don't rush into a partnership without examining every angle. Ask the following questions:
- Are they motivated by goals similar to yours?
- Are they self-reliant and also able to be part of a team?

- Are they emotionally stable?
- Do they bring out the best in you?
- Would you trust them completely?

And more cynically, but also worth considering:

- What skills/experience do they bring to the group (web design, database management, public speaking etc)?
- Do they have contacts that will help raise money, create exposure, offer organisational support and win sponsors?

Girlfriends, Boyfriends, Husbands and Wives

You may be thinking of taking on a project with your partner, whether it is a girlfriend or boyfriend, husband or wife. In normal life you look to one another as the first sounding board for ideas, the first shoulder to cry on and for the first hug of celebration. This may make your partner the perfect companion for the physical and emotional ordeal you are contemplating. But, you also know how to antagonise each other in a blink and how to wind each other up to distraction and, as if having been schooled by ten year old brothers, how to inspire temporary hatred and frustration with a hand gesture. In view of all of this, your partner could equally well be the last person or the only person you would want next to you when you are at your lowest ebb, stinking of three days sweat and running out of money, with 30 miles of desert before the next village and darkness falling fast.

It may seem as if you are making a decision about how strong your relationship is, but this is not so. Rather, you are making a decision about what kind of people you both are. Are you both, independently, motivated for the right reasons?

Tim Garrett, Andy Brown and his girlfriend, Suzanne, were a team of cyclists motivated by the same dissatisfaction with their lifestyle and a common awareness of injustices in the world. They set out from Sydney to cross Australia, Africa and South America for Practical Action, who used the £35,000 they raised to support training programmes for farmers and pastoralists in the Turkana region Kenya. When Andy and Suzanne planned to take on the 16,000 km, they were together and it seemed like a perfect venture for them both. But when they finally set out they had separated and Suzanne had a new boyfriend. In Andy's words the trip was "miserable and full of arguments for three months". This project of a lifetime was being defined by their relationship, which could not support the emotional strain of the daily grind. The three that arrived in Mombasa became two as they climbed back onto their bikes towards Tanzania. It was Suzanne who had to decide to return to England and who missed out on the rest of an incredible journey around the world.

Recruiting Specialist Challenge Members

If there is a major aspect of the challenge that you do not feel confident about, or you simply need more members of the team, then you may have to advertise.

"There is a basic rule that most professional and experienced expeditioners stick to: avoid groups of three. This applies to teams or groups of any kind, because within a team of three there will normally always be one strong friendship that overrides the other two and decisions become harder to make and problems more difficult to overcome."

James Winton, Explorer and Adventurer

Special skills and experience become more important as your project grows in ambition so do not be afraid to seek out those with the necessary qualifications who may be willing to give you their time. Doctors, nurses, drivers, photographers, journalists and all sorts of well-paid professionals take time out from their day jobs to help worthwhile causes such as Médecins sans Frontières and VSO. They gain a new perspective on their work and perhaps a renewed sense of self-worth. The opportunity to become involved in a project like yours, without the responsibility of organising it, may be exactly what they are looking for.

The Role

- Exactly how will they help you achieve your aims?
- What is their general role within the project?
- What will they be doing in this capacity on a day to day basis?
- Can you pay their expenses and if so how much will they cost you?
- If they will be providing a professional skill for no money what happens if they a) do not fulfil their role b) want to give up?

The Person

- What skills do they have to have and what level of proof (qualifications, references) will you require from them?
- What kind of person will fit in with your group?
- Are you concerned about their interest in the cause?

Administration Tips

Insurance

Most companies offer cover for adventurous activities, but check that the policy protects you against loss in every aspect of what you are going to be doing as well as for all of your equipment. You may need individual policies for specialist or particularly expensive equipment. Keep receipts and an equipment list with all relevant model/serial numbers and take photos of everything before you leave.

Permits and VISAS

Plan and research all your requirements early on. If you are taking a support vehicle, then investigate what is required at every border and apply well in advance of departure if necessary. Large and specialist equipment, such as bicycles, kayaks and video cameras, may need particular permits. Certain activities, such as mountain climbing, may also require official permission. The Foreign Office (www.fco.gov.uk) website provides details of what is required and more information can be found through the embassies of the relevant countries.

An Admin Document

Prepare an admin document listing all your insurance details, medical particulars, equipment information, card and bank details and a copy of your itinerary. Each member in the group as well as a family member or trusted friend at home should have a copy, to be looked after carefully.

Health

On top of the physical conditioning and nutritional advice given in section 5, you need to be aware of good expeditional medical practice.

Dr Sean Hudson, Medical Director of Expedition Medicine, a renowned expert in his field and an experienced expeditions medic with Across the Divide, accompanies you through this section.

- Put together a first aid kit with the advice of a doctor with expedition experience. Ensure the whole team know how and when to use the kit.
- Consider including an expedition medic in your team
- All members of the group should have basic first-aid training and one member should have been through more advanced medical expedition training, appropriate to the needs and environment of your project

"If a member of the team is on medication for a particular condition, ensure they bring twice the medication they will need for the trip. The expedition leader or medic can take responsibility for half the medication, in case some is lost or damaged. Furthermore, in malaria areas, ideally all expeditioners should be taking the same antimalarials, so if medication is lost there's always plenty of spare ."

Sean Hudson, Medical Director, Expedition Medicine

- Research the health risks of the environment and ensure that all the necessary vaccinations are planned for well in advance (Travax, Foreign Office and the CIA have great

websites). Do not assume that all group members already have received the basic course of immunisations that most children do in the UK.
- Research the health needs of every individual member: this should include group discussion and knowledge of allergies, medication, chronic illnesses, relevant medical histories, as well as more sensitive issues such as psychiatric problems.
- Travellers diarrhoea is still the most common traveller's illness. The risks can be minimised by maintaining the highest standards of hygiene possible

"Have a signed report from their GP if possible. Expedition medics should always repeat consultations in the field as participants are sometimes unwilling to divulge certain issues and new problems may have developed since your first meeting."

Sean Hudson, Medical Director, Expedition Medicine

and taking note of the good practice advice in the Nutrition section. Consider carrying antibiotics for treatment of enteric gastroenteritis.
- Hygiene, hydration, nutrition, rest and acclimatisation are the key factors in maintaining your health.
- Information - Carry a medical handbook relevant to your environment and activity. This will help you be aware of particular risks, prevention methods and acceptable means of self-diagnoses and treatment.
- Carry contact details of local medical professionals and helplines at home. There are invaluable 24-hour help lines for altitude and cold related illness, diving medicine and tropical medicine.

1. Acclimatisation

Your body is capable of dealing with a wide range of extreme environments, but it must be given time to adapt. Avoid exposing your body to any shocks and you will minimise the risks of these changes. This is particularly important for altitude, extreme heat/cold and levels of physical exertion.

High-Altitude

High-Altitude Sickness/ Acute Mountain Sickness (AMS) is a serious issue for those undertaking a challenge at high-altitude (approximately above 2,500m). If you have any history of heart problems or ill health or plan to exercise at high altitude for the first time consult your doctor.

Avoiding High-Altitude Sickness

The key is acclimatisation, which means that you must take your time travelling to higher altitudes. As you travel, your body will start to adapt to the reduced oxygen levels (hypoxia), but this happens gradually. If you ascend too far above the level to which you are acclimatised then there is not enough oxygen for your body to function properly, so you suffer symptoms of AMS.

Avoiding High-Altitude Sickness

- If possible, you should spend at least one night at an intermediate elevation below 3000 metres.
- At altitudes above 3000 metres (10,000 feet), your sleeping elevation should not increase more than 300-500 metres (1000-1500 feet) per night.
- Every 1000 metres (3000 feet) you should spend a second night at the same elevation.

Identifying High-Altitude Sickness

- First signs: light-headedness, headache, weakness, loss of appetite, nausea or vomiting, difficulty sleeping. If you experience any of these you need to return to a lower altitude and rest until the symptoms end.
- Advanced signs: difficulty breathing (even at rest), confusion and disorientation, coughing. An immediate return to lower altitude and medical attention is required at this stage.

Thomas Dietz, International Society for Mountain Medicine

At high altitude it is crucial that you prepare and plan thoroughly to reduce the risks of high-altitude sickness. (photo: Charity Challenge)

2. Safety and Risk Assessment

A risk assessment is a logical and detailed examination of what could cause harm to the team. For health, safety, legal and insurance reasons, this is an important part of any challenge expedition. It involves analysing potential hazards and matching them with the control measures that you have/will have in place.

FIRST - Divide the project up into its various parts and assess the risks:
- The needs and abilities of the team
- The activity you will be undertaking
- The environment (terrain, altitude, weather, disease, medical facilities, communications, society/politics)

THEN - Address each risk with corresponding control factors to minimise each one.
- Make every member aware of the risk assessment that has been carried out and all the control factors
- Plan for the worst case scenario and establish and practice procedures for emergencies
- Accumulate relevant health and safety contacts – local and international
- Make thorough contingency plans, for example let friends/contacts/rescue services/authorities know your route and schedule in as much detail as possible and take an emergency signalling/communication device
- Allow elements of your risk assessment to be flexible to the changing needs of the group and the environment.
- Consider the implications of the risks that you are taking against every aspect of the project, particularly its overall success, the safety of the group and the reputation of your charity, your sponsors and challenge projects as a whole.

Despite the heat of the Tanzanian Highlands, Duncan Brown wears his helmet and gloves, substantially reducing his risks of minor and major injury from falls such as this one. Make sure that you buy, use and wear the right equipment. (photo Jonny Polonsky)

Risk Assessment - Burnside River Expedition 2001

A risk assessment is a process which quantifies the hazards in a given situation and seeks to identify ways to reduce the likelihood of the hazard causing harm.

HAZARD	STEPS TAKE TO REDUCE RISK
River	• Study river guide • Gather anecdotal information about the river • Gather information about annual changes and the effects of the current climate on river conditions
Wildlife (Bears, Wolves, etc.)	• Cook away from campsite • Run a clean and tidy camp • Employ principles from Bear Awareness course
Environment	• Food - pre-packed using a supplier known to the team members. • Shelter - A good quality tent backed up by lightweight bivi bags, and a tarp or bivi sheet, which could be used if the tent was damaged or lost. • Hydration - A constant theme throughout the day for both members of the team was checking food and drink levels to ensure team members were in top form at all times. • Pace - Goal setting for each day of the journey was flexible to ensure that environmental conditions and team needs were taken into account. • Spare food - Although it was calculated that the journey would take up to 16 days, sufficient food was taken to allow for bad weather days or additional rest days if required.
Crisis Management	• Next of Kin details submitted to the Heart of Kent Hospice • Rescue - would be from RCMP and was organized through the hire of a Personal Location Beacon, this involved logging the journey with the RCMP on arrival in country at Yellowknife. • The journey was also logged with the Float Plane Company and Outfitters with expected due dates
Transport	• Reputable floatplane operators and international carriers for the flights were chosen.

2. The Expedition

Once the challenge is underway and you are on the road it is easy to forget all sense of organisation and rely upon the preparations you have already made. However, your tough new challenge lifestyle can be made less stressful by giving the logistics and adminstration of the trip some time and consideration. Once you have system in place for each area of the expedition, you will be able to concentrate on the challenge at hand.

The Team

Maintaining strong and workable team relations is vital to the success of the challenge. It will undoubtedly come under stress, but if you deal with this in the right way and enable the pressure to be relieved, then it will not endanger your overall success.

- Once you have assembled the team, spend time together and learn as much as possible about each other's characters
- Consider the skills that are necessary for your expedition and ensure that they are well covered within the group – if not, then training must take place before you set off. See the reference section for recommended organisations.
- Distribute roles within the team fairly and as precisely as possible.
- Every member should participate in decision-making; short and long-term objectives should be explicit and accepted by all.
- On a daily basis, all members must be aware of distance to be covered, the route, the destination and all planned stops and breaks.
- Appoint a leader – not necessarily the strongest character, but someone who can be relied upon in times of crisis and is impartial during discussions.
- Listen to each other and be aware of strengths, weaknesses and sensitivities.
- Hold regular meetings to air problems, rather than letting them build up into major obstacles.

Leadership

In most cases the leader of the group will be the individual who initiated the idea. The ownership of that idea will give that individual the greatest vested interest. A leader may also be the individual with the greatest experience, or one may naturally emerge during the very early stages of a project. Chris Loynes in his "Leadership and Teamwork" chapter for the RGS Expedition Handbook lays out three types of skills which a good leader should have:

- Hard Skills – technical skills relating to the activity; safety, planning and administrative skills and experience; knowledge of the environment.
- Soft skills – good communication skills; understanding of individual and group psychology

- Meta-skills – creativity; judgement; problem-solving skills

Once a leader has been established, their success will depend largely on the above assets. They should also be able to:

- Develop an in-depth knowledge of each individual's skills and needs
- Match these with the skills and experience that will be required during the challenge
- Take responsibility for the safety of the group and carry out thorough risk assessments (pages 199-200)
- Develop a consultation and participation process for decision-making that is efficient, effective and accepted, not simply democratic
- Communicate decisions with reasoning, not excuses
- Delegate control according to skills and experience
- For every decision bear in mind these main factors: the successful completion of the challenge and the experience, development and safety of the group

Top Tips: Expedition Essentials

1. Route, Navigation and Schedule

- Make sure maps are up-to-date and suitably scaled for your purposes. Be familiar with the map's key

- Plan routes as far in advance as possible, allowing time to research its demands and develop contacts along the way
- Even if you are following roads or marked routes, take a compass and/or GPS equipment to complement your map
- Make sure that everyone in the group is aware of the day's route and schedule and has the means to navigate themselves to a meeting point if they become separated
- Take weather and terrain into consideration when planning routes
- Talk to locals to find out more information about your route
- Plan to arrive at your destination with sufficient hours of light for cooking and setting up camp
- Schedule rest stops so as to divide up the day efficiently, rather than just stopping when you are tired

2. Environmental Impact

- Minimise the environmental impact of your expedition by a) making the assessment and reduction of such impact a priority and b) appointing a member of the team to check and monitor these issues
- Remember that the bigger the expedition, the greater the environmental impact
- Divide your project into general areas and minimise your impact for each. For example:

- Travelling – use public transport or efficient vehicles; stick to marked/designated routes and pathways
- Shopping, eating and drinking – buy products with minimal packaging and remove any unnecessary wrapping; buy local rather than imported goods; cook food using a liquid fuel, which increases efficiency and reduces waste; filter or treat water rather than buying bottles
- Accommodation/Camping – choose hotels/hostels which have environmental policies and initiatives; leave your camping area as you found it; burn combustible waste in controlled conditions and dispose of non-combustible waste in a major town or city; bury human waste away from water sources/supplies.

Find examples of kit lists and recommended retailers for maps and equipment on the website, as well as resources for more detailed and specialist expedition advice.

3. Camping

- The site should be close to water but away from animal drinking places; use cleared and level ground, but avoid floodplains; look for protection from wind
- Tents should be pitched with their noses to the wind

- A latrine should be dug away from the water supply and not upwind from the camp
- Ensure that fires are permitted in the area and build them a safe distance from tents, but close enough to help reduce insect presence
- Wash pots downstream from where water is being collected and do not use detergents
- Leave the area through which you have passed exactly as you found it: carry your rubbish until it can be properly disposed of; burn toilet paper and bury human waste; thoroughly clean up and cover your fire area.

4. Equipment

- Produce a kit list specific to your activity and its environment
- For brands, take advice from independent reviewers or specialist outdoor shops (also see Recommended Retailers on the website)
- Do not use overtly military-style clothing or equipment
- On self-sufficient expeditions pack weight is your priority – buy light and essential equipment
- Your camping equipment needs to be suitable for the environment
- Road test all equipment thoroughly – nothing should be used for the first time during the expedition
- Make sure that all your equipment is covered by your insurance policy

FINANCES

Being financially organised and totally transparent is essential for the success of your project. Supporters are entitled to see that the money you raise is going exactly where it should. Many grant giving bodies will simply not consider you if you do not have a detailed and realistic income and expenditure budget to show them. On a long and demanding challenge expedition you need the confidence of knowing that your finances are in good shape. You also need to be flexible enough to cope with emergencies and you will need contingency plans.

The Project Budget

The preparation of a budget is one of the first jobs for all projects. It may simply consist of a pair of trainers, an entrance fee and some estimated postage and printing costs. Or it may have to cover everything from inoculations and sun cream to satellite telephones and flying doctor cover. Whatever its scope, plan it, research it and draw it up meticulously. If you cannot cover your own costs and you are including a contribution to expenditure in the donations, then your budget must make this clear (more details on page **). Supporters should only be asked to provide for your absolute essential needs – equipment, food, water, accommodation – and each of these at their most basic level.

Expenditure

Your main budget document will include a breakdown of all your proposed costs. This expenditure budget is obviously a fluid document: some elements will prove more expensive than estimated while sponsorship and gifts in kind can bring down costs. Whatever happens, it is vital to keep this budget up to date for the following reasons:

1. Accountability

Good accountability will help you appear professional and organised to donors, who may even ask to see the project's financial records. These may also come under scrutiny if you find yourself faced with a large unpredictable expense that significantly affects the amount of money you can give to your chosen organisation. In this case, criticism can be quickly deflected with a comprehensive and accurate accounts document.

Furthermore, if you have not been able to cover all of your costs yourself, you are essentially asking the charity to bear them. You are working on their behalf as a voluntary fundraiser and incurring costs which you are asking to be covered from the money you raise. Consequently, it is only right and fair, and may even be obligatory, to provide a detailed breakdown of all of these expenses.

 Always keep receipts - For all money spent on the project, from the purchase of stamps for fundraising letters to the buying of specialist equipment, keep the receipts and make a note of that expenditure.

2. Confidence in resources

At times there will be an enormous amount of things occupying your mind. When combined with the unrelenting physical exertion, these will become magnified. If you are able to keep track of your resources, your average expenditure and your projected expenditure in one organised document, then whatever financial trouble the project finds itself in, you will at least be able to know what to expect and how to prepare for it. It may seem easier to just forget about money, spend on credit and sort it out when you reach the end, but this could end in disaster, when you find out how little your efforts have produced for the charity. Establishing a very basic accounting system for the road before you start as well as a detailed budget will allow more confidence to plan ahead and make you able to relax more easily when you take time off.

3. Group Relations

As a group, a sound consensus over finances is imperative. There will probably be differing motivations and attitudes towards the finances of the project within the team, so having a budget and keeping proper records of expenditure removes some of the potential for conflict. Even if you have to get everyone to sign agreements, which may seem totally at odds with the spirit and nature of the project, it may pre-empt frustration and resentment.

Expedition Accounting

Under the stress and strain of daily exercise, and in the context of trying to reach a target for charity, money can become a constant worry. There needs to be a system in place suited to the kind of situations you are going to be in and each member needs their own resources.

- Divide the route up into points at which you have access to money
- Do not rely on ifs and maybes - carry enough money to keep you going until the next point, including emergencies
- Research the best foreign currency to carry and the credit cards that are accepted locally
- Take a variety of financial resources – cash, travellers cheques of different currencies, VISA and Mastercard credit cards
- Have someone at home who can cable money to you if necessary
- Keep everyday money separate from your main cash resources
- If you have to carry a lot of cash then divide it up into smaller amounts in safe places – that includes being safe from damage
- The Treasurer can keep a notebook of expenditure and be given all relevant receipts
- Take account of unpredictable expenses – medical attention, repairs, border crossings, tourist registration fees, insurance etc
- PLAN AHEAD – getting stuck with no money and no means of accessing any can jeopardise the entire project

Damion Walker celebrates in style after finishing the gruelling Marathon des Sables

Documenting

Making good records of your project is really important and should be done as thoroughly as possible by everyone undertaking a challenge. The benefits of these records will primarily be two fold. Firstly, photographs, diaries and video footage of a remarkable and perhaps one off achievement will be very personally valuable. You will never regret making good records of your challenge. Secondly, your chosen charity is always in need of interesting material to promote their challenges and their organisation. You become a very positive advert for their work, so the more comprehensive and qualitative your records the more value it has to them.

Documenting the challenge

These two basic benefits apply to challenges and projects of every type. For those who are aiming higher in the work they want to do for their charity there are further reasons for dedicating time and resources to recording your undertaking thoroughly and professionally. Your aim is to inspire and inform, and the materials you produce can be used to further this very effectively:

• Material for your website
• Part of e-mails, newsletters and thank you letters
• Multi-media awareness presentations during and after the challenge
• Creative material for fundraising events
• Exhibitions and displays
• Basis for press, television and radio articles
• Production into documentaries, features or short films
• Editing into published diaries

Photography

Photographs are an important part of any holiday or trip as a reminder, a way of sharing and a record of your travels. During an endurance challenge their relevance is not just personal, but can fulfil so many important roles. From the first moment that you decide to take on a challenge you should be taking photos.

Digital technology suits your needs very well. Most obviously, you can take as many photos as you like, which given your activities, will be very handy. Secondly, you will be using the photographs for a variety of purposes that will require the photos to be in digital format anyway – websites, e-mails, presentations for example. Converting rolls of film to CD is quite expensive, although it is very possible.

Travel Photography Tips

• Take all your equipment with you – do not rely upon getting reliably high quality items where you are going, including spare batteries, films and memory cards.
• Treat your film/memory cards like gold dust – they are invaluable.
• Carry your films in your hand luggage to minimise risk from damage to unexposed films from x-ray machines
• Get a test roll of film developed locally occasionally to check quality.
• Send home films/memory cards regularly if you can ensure their safety

Equipment

The best advice for camera equipment comes from specialist photography shops, especially privately owned outlets, run by knowledgeable enthusiasts. Describe your needs as specifically as possible.

Things to remember:

- If you are going to carry equipment with you during the challenge it needs to be light and durable
- High spec compact cameras will give excellent results in most situations, but give you slightly less control in more difficult conditions
- If you have room for a zoom lens, then for SLR cameras (Single Lens Reflex) a general purpose lens of 24-85mm is recommended and for DSLR (Digital Single Lens Reflex) a general purpose of 18-70mm should suit your needs
- You need to be able to protect the camera and equipment from the elements while also allowing quick access.
- A monopod can be light and manageable and adds to the quality of the pictures.
- Invest in a basic cleaning kit.
- Take a variety of film for different conditions – all purpose 200iso, low light 400iso, high light 100iso.
- Take plenty of spare memory cards for digital cameras as well as a digital wallet.
- Make sure that the equipment is covered in your insurance.

Practise with your equipment before you leave so that using it well becomes second nature. You might just have a split second to take the picture that defines and promotes the entire project.

Technical Tips

- Take a number of shots of important moments with different levels of exposure and from different angles.

Cameraman Jonny Polonsky chooses an apt moment for a mid-challenge interview (photo: Jono Felix)

- Give yourself time to focus properly or allow the auto-focus a moment to do its work.
- The best light for landscape shots is normally just after sunrise or before sun set.
- The flash can throw light onto shadows in any conditions – even in the midday sun – so don't be afraid to use it at any time.
- Portrait shots are often most striking with a plain background with the main source of light coming from one side of the picture.

What to Shoot

Ideas for Photographs and Video

- Preparation - Training, plotting the route, fundraising, events
- Important stages - Setting off, half-way, finishing
- Participants - Leave empty shots of stunning scenery to the pros – put a cyclist or a runner in there and it is an original and interesting image or cut-away. Include the participants or willing subjects in the vast majority of all photos
- Changes in environment - Every time the scenery or surroundings change substantially
- Context - Landmarks, road signs, oceans, mountains, deserts, bridges etc
- Crises - It may not seem appropriate but these shots are vital to your story
- Emotion - No matter if positive or negative, emotional moments make for powerful shots. Include humorous, sad and tense moments.
- Subjects - If you are interviewing people, visiting schools or being hosted by particular organisations then a visual record to sit alongside your other recordings or descriptions is vital (remember to take names and cross check).
- Sponsors - Shots of products in action are valuable to existing and potential sponsors
- Articles - Shots for specialist sport

(Photo: Charity Challenge)

magazines, travel sections, the adventure press etc.

- Everyday challenge life - Warming up, camping and eating may seem mundane to you but it is essential that you can show others every aspect of the challenge
- Regularity - Bursts of footage or photos at a particular time should be avoided, so think about shooting all the time, rather than just at remarkable moments.

Video

Video footage is a great way of recording and sharing your adventure, regardless of its size, but before charging blindly into investing in expensive equipment, be realistic about your project's potential. Central to these decisions must be the fulfilment of your main aims – raising money and awareness for your charity. For a large charity expedition, filming a documentary, selling it to a production company on your return and reaping financial and publicity rewards appears to be an end worth pursuing, no matter the cost.

However, you need to look realistically at the potential of your project, as the equipment for such an undertaking is expensive and complex. Ask yourself the following questions about your appeal:

- Does your project offer something original?
- As an individual or a group are you potentially interesting to the public?
- Are the conditions you will experience extreme enough to warrant large scale popular interest?

And in terms of the project's resources:
- Will you have room within your schedule to invest a lot of time in recording footage?
- Will you be able to carry the necessary equipment?
- Is it feasible to take a back up team that can dedicate itself to filming?
- Can you afford to cover the costs of the equipment and materials if nothing comes of the footage?

Equipment

Here are some suggestions for essential equipment if you intend to record high-quality footage".

- Camera - A 3 chip digital camera is the minimum technical specification for TV quality footage (e.g. Sony PDX 10). If TV is not a consideration then a single chip camera is sufficient.
- Lenses - Wide angle and filters make a big difference to a small camera, particularly if you are shooting in bright light, particularly desert or snow conditions.
- Audio - Sound quality is vital and poor audio has a huge effect on the impact and interest that the film might inspire. On-board microphones are very rarely up to scratch, so invest in a good quality external microphone (e.g. Senheiser 416).
- Tripod - Even the steadiest handed operator will benefit from a light-weight tripod/monopod for fixed shots and interviews.
- Tapes - Lots of Mini DV tapes are needed.
- Cleaning equipment - Can-air, air-brush, lens cloth, gaffer tape (head cleaner cassettes can often do more damage than good, so avoid them).

Technique

The standard of your filming technique is vital. Follow these techinical tips from experienced cameraman and producer Ollie Steeds, director of iNOMAD.

General Techniques

- Lighting - Use natural light where possible, best times are early morning and late afternoon
- Audio - Use good headphones to check audio levels constantly. With background noise, e.g. a fan, make sure you get a shot of the fan and the clear audio
- Zoom - Keep zooming to a minimum - if you want a closer shot, get closer to the subject
- The Line - Imagine there is a 180° line running through the subject and never cross it
- Tripod – If possible ensure all shots are 'locked-off' on a tripod.

Interviews

- Framing – Film medium headshot (i.e. head and shoulders) and head-shots for most telling/important parts. Subject should be talking into space, not into the camera
- Zoom - Only zoom at moments of intensity. Zoom to fix a new shot when the subject is not talking
- Eye-Line - The subject's eye line should be one third from the top. The camera should be set at subject's eye-level
- Interviews with translations - Ensure that a) the subject and translator are recorded on separate audio channels b) the translator does not talk at the same time as the subject
- Audio
  - minimise background noise by i) using a quiet location ii) ensuring the mic is closer to subject
  - ensure that the subject is not interrupted whilst talking
  - keep mics and cables out of shot
- Two-way interviews – You will need:
  - cutaways of the interviewer reacting to the subject
  - fixed shots of the interviewer asking the questions
  - separate audio channels for the subject and interviewee
  - cutaways – over the shoulders of each interviewee
- Subject matter – remember to ensure that you have picture of what the subject talks about – e.g. if they're talking about chickens, you'll need pictures of the chickens in question.
- Cutaways (c/a) – Standard c/as include hand gestures, close-ups of eyes, interesting clothing etc. Experiment with angles (high, low, reverses, moves). Film a minimum of 10 seconds per c/a.
- Contextual shots - Film wide angles and the subject at work or in their natural environment

Other Essential Areas

- Diaries – Think 'Big Brother' and make them personal, emotional and part of your story-line
- Special Effects (FX) – Some cameras have inbuilt FX. Don't use them
- Landscape & General Views – These are mainstay of most films. Shoot them regularly, using tripod fixed shots – wides, mediums, close-ups - with pans if possible.
- Flora & Fauna – For best light and activity film early and late in the day
- People – Film fixed shots, framed portraits, people at work etc

The Edit

Aim to edit two promotional shorts: one for potentially interested production companies and one for awareness purposes. The latter is essential as a tool for building upon the great work you have done for your charity and it will prove very popular amongst your friends, families and sponsors.

The Awareness Short

Produce a short film that will inspire and inform.

- Introduce the main protagonists
- Demonstrate the purpose and the cause clearly. Show the nature of the issue your charity is addressing, what their work is and how you are contributing
- Portray your main challenge activities succinctly and imaginatively e.g. cycling, camping, cooking, meeting local people
- Illustrate the endurance elements as emotively as possible i.e. exhausted expressions, extreme conditions etc.
- Finish with shots of celebration, relief and some interaction with your cause e.g. a diary about what it means to you, an interview with someone involved, cut-aways of relevant scenes

The Promotional Short

Produce a short film to "sell" your challenge to a production company.

- You are selling a story, with a beginning, middle and end and which needs to take the audience through a variety of emotions. Put together either a shortened version of this story OR an exciting chapter of it

- A good story relies on its characters, so give your most interesting protagonists time to establish themselves and demonstrate why they are worth watching
- Pull out your most dramatic moments – emotionally, physically and environmentally.
- Leave the audience wanting more. Ask a neutral party if they would want to watch this material for 30/60 minutes.

The Sell

When you have put together a promotional short, research the potential interest carefully and try to develop contacts within the industry. Avoid sending unsolicited or unexpected packages, as they will disappear into a heap of tapes and DVDs. Write a summary document that accompanies the short. It should include:

- A title and a brief and enticing outline
- A more detailed breakdown of the type of footage or story you have told, including brief biographies of your main characters
- Technical details – equipment specifications; methods and techniques; experience of camera operator

 Once a production company has bought your footage, they will naturally, unless specifically agreed otherwise, be at liberty to do anything they want with it. This means that your tremendously exciting and well meaning expedition could become a story of bitter emotional chaos, in which four hateable stereotypes trek angrily across several countries. Never underestimate the power of the edit.

Audio

The aim of making audio recordings is more focussed than either video or photography, as its appeal will be limited almost exclusively to radio or personal consumption. This, however, does not limit its potential impact. Radio stations are the most likely to take an interest in the project and give it air time. Radio pieces with a combination of post-mortem interviews, on the road updates, stories and recordings make very successful programmes. Such programmes also present a clearer benefit in terms of awareness for your cause, as listeners to talk radio stations tend to be more interested in local, national and international issues and events. Instead of a constant battle with journalists and producers to emphasise more positive and topical aspects of the project, you will often be pushed by radio stations to show how relevant this cause is to their listeners and why they should be aware of it. Audio recordings also offer a far less complicated, costly and risky investment than camera footage and may also be more suited to the scope of the project.

If you have made the decision not to record video footage of television quality, which is a substantial commitment, audio recordings are certainly worth consideration. Even just a weekend of walking would contain initial expectation, tiredness, bits of frustration, plenty of humour and final scenes of relief and exhilaration. All of these moments of emotion can be recorded very quickly and simply, and could very feasibly form the basis of a short article on community or local radio. On solo projects, or those with very limited means and resources, audio recordings could prove extremely powerful. Descriptions of scenes and events by those within them are very often more emotive and illustrative than pictures, as they portray more than what can be seen, describing also what is being felt.

Equipment

- Minidisk players are currently the easiest and cheapest means of making audio recordings – compact, easy to use and durable. MP3 recorders are the future, but still fairly expensive.
- A good quality microphone is vital and there are three options: mono mics are easy to use and get the best quality of speech recordings; stereo mics are more common, less expensive and are more sensitive to actuality and background noises (which can be an advantage and disadvantage); tie-clip\lapel mics are not sufficient as your only mic, but are cheap and handy as an extra for interviews or as a spare.

Technique

- Be polite but confident – you have to get near to what you are recording to make it worth listening to, so don't feel shy about getting to the front of a crowd or asking someone if you can hold a microphone near them.
- When you are interviewing hold the microphone up and about 30cm from the person speaking and try and position yourself so you don't have to keep on moving it back and forth.

Written Records

On a personal level, you will have a record of your thoughts upon an extraordinary event in your life. The project as a whole will benefit hugely from notes of what happens, what goes wrong and what is successful. If you ever decide to take on another challenge, then you will have details of your experiences. The more challenge fundraising experience that can be accumulated, recorded and shared, the less time and effort is wasted in mistaken initiatives in the future.

There is also the potential of being printed. The possibilities for this are almost endless, as thousands of newspapers, magazines, journals, newsletters, annual reviews and books look for imaginative material to fill their pages.

Keeping a Diary

- If you have never written a diary then try and make it a habit. During the planning, fundraising and training stages keep it in a place that will allow you to use it as part of your daily routine.
- If you cannot maintain one every day or very regularly, then make sure that you make a note of important events or experiences.
- During the challenge itself, consider keeping it in a plastic resealable bag with a pencil and sharpener.
- Use it to collect the names and contact details of everyone you meet, as well as the date and context of the meeting.

Andy Brown and Tim Garratt at the end of their 16,000km journey around the world, raising money for Practical Action. Having kept a journal throughout the trip they arrived home and wrote Discovery Road, a joint account of their remarkable journey across three continents. The book was published by Eye Books in 1997 and is currently in its 4th Edition, having sold over 30,000 copies. Read an extract from the book on the page 218.

'Will Mr. Ray Johnson please report to the information booth immediately,' a woman's shrill voice boomed over the tannoy. 'Mrs. Johnson has been waiting for him for over two hours.' A loud cheer went up from the crowd into the clear morning sunshine.

'He's in the bloody pub missus,' someone shouted.

'Piss off and leave him in peace!' called another.

The crowd roared its laughter, high on the camaraderie of people having fun.

Suzanne, Andy and I had chosen Bondi Beach as the starting point of our journey. Unfortunately, so had the 'City to Surf' half marathon and we found ourselves competing for space with several thousand runners, back up teams, spectators and hot dog vans. The race had started at Sydney Opera House two hours before and was finishing here on the grassy esplanade overlooking the beach.

A clown, complete with red plastic nose, baggy yellow trousers and red braces, jogged past juggling multi-coloured balls. Minutes later a large, black gorilla loped towards me. I clapped him on his way.

'G'day,' came a grunted greeting as he passed.

I stripped down to black cycling shorts for a ceremonial dip and Suzanne paddled amongst the white breakers of the Pacific Ocean to fill a miniature plastic gin bottle with water.

'It's symbolic,' she explained with a smile. 'Coast to coast, east to west. This water will travel with me all the way to Perth where I'll set it free in the Indian Ocean'.

I was impressed, I would never have thought of something like that, but then girls are different aren't they.

Exhausted runners were still collapsing under the finishing clock as we lined up our bikes to start. This was the last time we would look so smart, if a little pasty-faced from too much British sunshine! Crisply ironed white T-shirts boldly stated our mission – 'CYCLE FOR I.T. – Biking Across 3 Continents for Intermediate Technology'. On the back of the shirts were green outline maps of Australia, Africa and South America and a dotted line indicating our intended route. Were these absurdly simple statements the product of supreme confidence or just foolish arrogance? I had a feeling we were soon to find out.

'This is weird,' said Andy. 'All these people are finishing their journeys and we're just beginning ours.'

We sat astride the bikes and held hands, Suzanne in the middle. Andy blessed the trip, 'Here's to success and friendship.'

'To success and friendship,' we chanted, shook hands and took our first pedal.

Three hundred metres down the road we stopped for lunch!

Index
and reference

Bibliography

Ackland, J. (2003) The Complete Guide to Endurance Training, A & C Black

Adreoni, J. (1989). Giving with impure altruism: applications to charity and ricardian equivalence. *Journal of Political Economy, 97*

Bates, Wells and Braithwaite and Voluntary Sector Development (2000) *The Fundraiser's Guide to the Law*, DSC, London

Bingham J and Hadfield J (2004) *Marathon Running for Mortals*, Rodale, London

Burian P and Caputo R (1999) *National Geographic Photography Field Guide*, National Geographic, London

Davis Smith J (1997) *The National Survey of Volunteering,* The National Centre for Volunteering, London

Dawkins R (1976) *The Selfish Gene*, Oxford University Press, Oxford

Foster V, Mourato S, Pearce D and Ozdermiraglu E (2000) *The Price of Virtue: The Economic Value of the Charitable Sector,* Edward Elgar, Cheltenham

Gifford N and Madden R (2004) *The Adventurous Traveller*, Constable & Robinson, London

Girard Eberle, S. (2000) Endurance Sports Nutrition, Human Kinetics Europe Ltd.

Gray F and Elsden S (2000) *Organising Special Events for Fundraising and Campaigning*, DSC/CAF, London

Morrison C (1997) *Donor Motivation*, Profunding, Newcastle Upon Tyne

NCVO (1998) *Blurred Vision - public trust in charities*, NCVO Research Quarterly, 1, January

NCVO (2000) *Coming Apart or Coming Together? New Findings on Social Participation and Trust in Britain*, NCVO Research Quarterly, 11.

Ryan, M. (2002) Sports Nutrition for Endurance Athletes, Velopress

Seebohar, B. (2004) Nutrition Periodization for Endurance Atheletes, Bell Publishing

Scott C (2001) *Adventure Motorcycling Handbook*, Trailblazer, Surrey

Stroud M (1999) *Survival of the Fittest,* Vintage, London

Catherine Walker (2002) *Altruism, Guilt and the Feel-Good Factor - Why do People Give to Charity?* in Catherine Walker and Cathy Pharoah (2002) A Lot of Give - Trends in Charitable Giving for 21st Century, CAF, Kent

Winser S (ed.) (2004), *Royal Geographic Society Expedition Handbook*, Profile, London

Expert Contributions from:

James Gero
www.sportsmedicineclinic.co.uk

James Gero formed Sports Medicine and Performance Enterprises in 1996. He spent much of his early teenage years running ultra marathons after completing his first 47 mile race at a tender age of 16. Since then he has raced in many marathons and ultra marathons ranging from 100 milers over harsh mountain terrain to multi day races such as the Marathon des Sables (a 7-day self-sufficient running event in the Sahara desert). He was the youngest athlete to race in this latter event when there were only a handful of competitors. He has helped hundreds of sportsmen and women reach their aspirations in their chosen events. Sports Medicine and Performance Enterprises now specialise in Sports Medicine and team welfare management for professional athletes and setting up sports medicine clinics, health clubs and corporate facilities.

Kathryn Bistany
www.corpotential.com

Kathryn Bistany, Founder and Managing Director of Corpotential Limited, left a career spanning 13 years in investment banking to re-train as a personal fitness trainer and sports therapist. After a serious injury and subsequent nutritional deficiencies, Kathryn re-trained in the field of nutrition with the University of Westminster in London and gained a Masters of Sports Nutrition from the University of Newcastle in Australia. Corpotential offers one-to-one consultations and group presentations.

Oliver Steeds
www.inomad.co.uk

Oliver Steeds is an explorer, author, public speaker, and founder of iNomad, an organisation dedicated to promoting exploration and communicating discovery. His expeditions have taken him to Indonesia, Malaysia, Vietnam, Syria and Jordan, Tibet, China and Mongolia. As a Mandarin speaker, his particular area of interest lies in China and the Far East.

Dr Sean Hudson
www.acrossthedivide.co.uk

Sean's first expedition was 1987, in Panama with John Blashford-Snell and Operation Raleigh, crossing the Darien Gap. He qualified as a doctor in 1993 and has worked in medicine, surgery, orthopaedics, anaesthetics, casualty and general practice, developing particular interests in expedition and sports medicine.

In 1998 when he went to work again for Raleigh as Chief Medic and Trek Leader. In 2000 he gained an M.Sc in Sports Medicine, with a speciality in hypothermia. During this time he was employed as a Medical Officer for Scottish Football Association. Sean has worked for Across the Divide Expeditions since 1998 and has been on 21 expeditions in 12 different countries.

In 2002 along with expedition medic Dr Caroline Knox he was instrumental in establishing Expedition Medicine Ltd which seeks to provide comprehensive training for medical professionals working as expedition medical officers and medics working in the remotest corners of the world.

Photograph Credits

Section Dividers

Why?	Robert Hadman
Choices	Charity Challenge
Fundraising	Michael Stanhope
Awareness	Tim Kitching
Documenting	Jonny Polonsky

Visit www.eye-books.com/BloodSweatandCharity for:

- Extra information and advice on charity challenges
- Free downloads to help you fundraise and train
- Full listings of charity challenge events in the UK and abroad
- Special offers and discounts
- More inspirational challenge profiles

Index